Contents

Introduction to the
toefl primary® Test   4

Actual Test 01   9

Actual Test 02   45

Actual Test 03   81

Answer Key   별책

Introduction to the toefl primary®

■ About toefl primary®

toefl primary®는 미국 ETS(Educational Testing Service)에서 개발한 영어학습 입문 단계의 글로벌 영어 인증 시험입니다. 영어를 모국어로 사용하지 않는 나라의 어린 학습자들을 대상으로 전반적인 영어 능력을 측정합니다.

toefl primary®는 PBT(Paper Based Tests) 방식의 toefl primary® Reading and Listening Test – Step 1 & Step 2와 iBT(internet Based Tests) 방식의 toefl primary® Speaking & Writing Test가 있습니다.

■ Test Options

- **toefl primary® Reading and Listening Test – Step 1**
  - 영어를 시작하는 초기 단계의 학습자 대상
  - 익숙한 환경(학교, 집, 운동장 등)에서 발생하는 일상생활과 밀접한 주제
  - 친숙한 인물 또는 사물과 관련된 기초 어휘와 표현
  - 일상생활에 필요한 간단한 지시문 및 학습 관련 짧은 지문 이해

- **toefl primary® Reading and Listening Test – Step 2**
  - 영어 의사소통 능력이 발달되고 있는 중급 단계의 학습자 대상
  - 일상생활의 범위를 넘어선 주제와 관련된 짧은 스토리와 대화 내용 이해
  - 기본적인 표현, 요구사항, 지시사항
  - 교과 기반의 지문 이해

- **toefl primary® Speaking Test**
  - 일상생활과 관련된 상황에서 필요한 의사소통을 하기 위한 말하기 능력 평가
  - 기본적인 감정과 의견 표현
  - 간단한 요청 또는 지시사항 표현
  - 사람, 사물, 동물, 장소, 활동 묘사
  - 간단한 사건을 시간 순서대로 설명

- **toefl primary® Writing Test**
  - 일상생활과 관련된 친숙한 주제에 대해 글로 소통하는 쓰기 능력 평가
  - 사람, 물건, 동물, 상황, 장소 및 활동에 대한 내용 이해
  - 간단한 상황을 순서대로 쓰기
  - 짧고 일관된 스토리 작성하기

■ Test Structure

toefl primary® Reading and Listening Test – Step 1

영역	문항 수	샘플 문항 수	총 문항 수	시험 시간	점수	등급
Reading	36	3	39	30분	100~109	1-4 등급 (☆로 표시)
Listening	36	5	41	30분	100~109	
Total	72	8	80	60분	200~218	

toefl primary® Reading and Listening Test – Step 2

영역	문항 수	샘플 문항 수	총 문항 수	시험 시간	점수	등급
Reading	36	1	37	30분	100~115	1-5 등급 (🏅로 표시)
Listening	36	3	39	35분	100~115	
Total	72	4	76	65분	200~230	

toefl primary® Speaking Test

영역	문항 수	시험 시간	점수	등급
Speaking	7~10	20분	1~27	1-5 등급 (🏅로 표시)

toefl primary® Writing Test

영역	문항 수	시험 시간	점수	등급
Writing	19	30분	1~17	1-4 등급 (🏅로 표시)

※ toefl primary® 공식 웹사이트: http://www.toeflyss.or.kr

Question Types

Ace the TOEFL Primary Step 1 – Reading

Part 1

한 개의 그림과 세 개의 보기가 주어집니다. 그림과 가장 잘 맞는 답을 고릅니다.

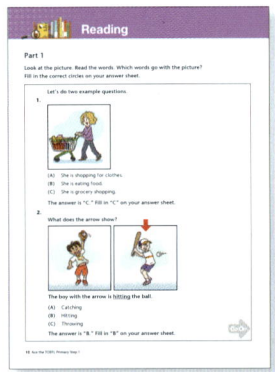

Part 2

2~3개의 문장으로 이루어진 짧은 설명과 세 개의 보기가 주어집니다. 설명에 해당하는 답을 고릅니다.

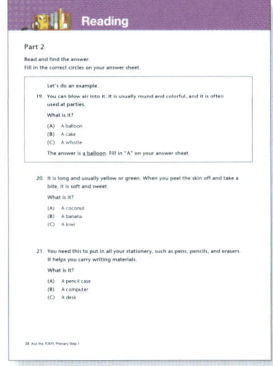

Part 3

이 파트에서는 두 종류의 글이 주어집니다. 첫 번째 글은 초대장, 일정, 광고, 포스터 등에 관한 것입니다. 주어진 글을 읽고 2~4개의 관련 질문에 답합니다.

두 번째 글은 이메일 또는 편지입니다. 주어진 글을 읽고 관련 질문 2개에 답합니다.

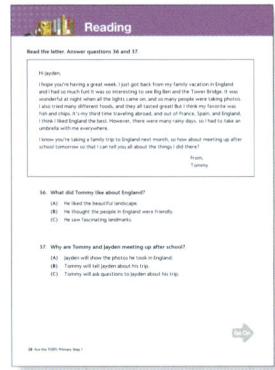

Ace the TOEFL Primary Step 1 – Listening

Part 1

세 개의 그림 보기가 주어지며, 들리는 문장에 해당되는 답을 고릅니다.

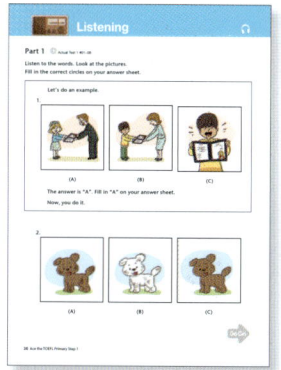

Part 2

세 개의 그림 보기가 주어지며, 들리는 지시사항을 가장 잘 따르거나 표현한 답을 고릅니다.

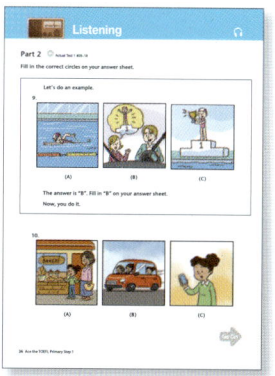

Part 3

두 사람이 주고받는 대화를 들은 후, 세 개의 보기 중 가장 자연스러운 대화를 고릅니다.

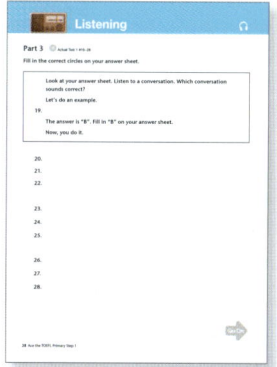

Part 4

두 사람의 대화를 들은 후, 대화에서 언급된 내용에 대한 질문에 답합니다.

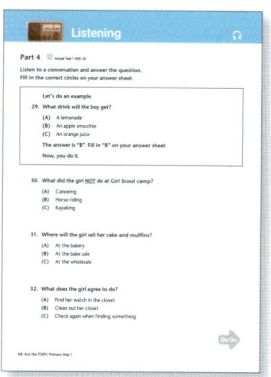

Part 5

전화 메시지를 들은 후, 전화를 건 목적이나 메시지에서 언급된 세부사항에 대한 질문에 답합니다.

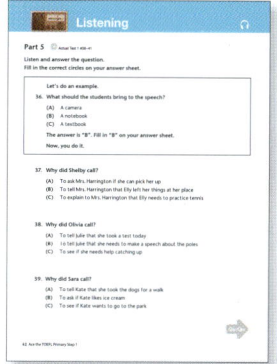

Actual Test 01

Reading

Part 1

Look at the picture. Read the words. Which words go with the picture?
Fill in the correct circles on your answer sheet.

Let's do two example questions.

1.

(A) She is shopping for clothes.
(B) She is eating food.
(C) She is grocery shopping.

The answer is "C." Fill in "C" on your answer sheet.

2.

What does the arrow show?

The boy with the arrow is <u>hitting</u> the ball.

(A) Catching
(B) Hitting
(C) Throwing

The answer is "B." Fill in "B" on your answer sheet.

Reading

3.

(A) Rhinoceros
(B) Bear
(C) Elephant

4.

(A) Comb
(B) Mirror
(C) Scissors

Reading

5.

(A) Walk
(B) Run
(C) Jump

6.

(A) Garden
(B) Kitchen
(C) Bedroom

Reading

7.

(A) Travel
(B) Rest
(C) Study

8.

(A) Bake
(B) Paint
(C) Study

Reading

9.

- (A) Knee
- (B) Ankle
- (C) Elbow

10.

- (A) Venus
- (B) Earth
- (C) Mars

Reading

11.

   (A) Huge
   (B) Tiny
   (C) Large

12.

   (A) The girl is talking.
   (B) The girl is sleeping.
   (C) The girl is dancing.

Reading

13.

(A) The tree is in front of the two children.

(B) The tree is between the two children.

(C) The tree is behind the two children.

14.

(A) There is a ruler.

(B) There are two calculators.

(C) There are five pencils.

Reading

15.

(A) The girl on the right has longer hair than the girl on the left.

(B) The girl on the left has longer hair than the girl on the right.

(C) The girl on the left has shorter hair than the girl on the right.

16.

(A) He is eating something hot.
(B) He is eating something sour.
(C) He is eating something sweet.

Reading

17.

(A) The boy is planting a tree.
(B) The girl is growing apples.
(C) The boy is picking apples.

18.

(A) The girl is getting ready to sleep.
(B) The girl is washing her blanket.
(C) The girl is folding her blanket.

Reading

Reading

Part 2

Read and find the answer.
Fill in the correct circles on your answer sheet.

Let's do an example.

19. You can blow air into it. It is usually round and colorful, and it is often used at parties.

    What is it?

    (A) A balloon
    (B) A cake
    (C) A whistle

    The answer is a balloon. Fill in "A" on your answer sheet.

---

20. It is long and usually yellow or green. When you peel the skin off and take a bite, it is soft and sweet.

    What is it?

    (A) A coconut
    (B) A banana
    (C) A kiwi

21. You need this to put in all your stationery, such as pens, pencils, and erasers. It helps you carry writing materials.

    What is it?

    (A) A pencil case
    (B) A computer
    (C) A desk

Reading

22. You are in math class. You need a calculator to solve questions but do not have one. You have to ask your friend.

    You are _____ a calculator from your friend.

    (A) lending
    (B) borrowing
    (C) sending

23. He is on a court with marked lines. He hits the ball hard with a racket, and the ball goes over the net.

    He is _____.

    (A) playing tennis
    (B) playing golf
    (C) playing hockey

24. When the weather is cold, people put these around their necks to keep warm. They come in various sizes, shapes, and colors.

    What are they?

    (A) Gloves
    (B) Scarves
    (C) Boots

Reading

25. They can make different sounds. They come in many shapes and sizes. People can make music with them.

    What are they?

    (A) Instruments
    (B) Candles
    (C) Paintings

26. The weather is not cold or hot. Many flowers and plants begin to grow, and everything feels new and fresh.

    It is _____.

    (A) summer
    (B) autumn
    (C) spring

27. You want to get information about a science project. You decide to go to a place with many books.

    You are going to _____.

    (A) a museum
    (B) a library
    (C) a coffee shop

Reading

Reading

Part 3

Fill in the correct circles on your answer sheet.

Read the science museum schedule 28 to 31.

Museum of Space Science

Dates	Floor	Activity	Entrance Fee
January 5th	1st Floor	**Explore the Solar System** - 3D planets exhibition - Learning about outer space	$10.00
January 16th	2nd Floor	**Build Rockets** - Making balloon rockets - Working with partners	$15.00
January 21st	2nd Floor	**Try on a Spacesuit** - Real astronaut spacesuits	$25.00
January 25th	3rd Floor	**View Models of Rockets** - Photo booth - Take pictures wearing spacesuits	$20.00

Reading

28. Which activity has the most expensive entrance fee?

    (A) Exploring the solar system
    (B) Building rockets
    (C) Trying on a spacesuit

29. When can people learn about the universe?

    (A) January 5th
    (B) January 16th
    (C) January 25th

30. On which floor can people put on a spacesuit?

    (A) 1st Floor
    (B) 2nd Floor
    (C) 3rd Floor

31. Which activity needs people working together?

    (A) Viewing models of rockets
    (B) Exploring the solar system
    (C) Building rockets

Reading

Read the sign. Answer questions 32 to 35.

Attention All Students!

We're excited to announce this year's Talent Show!

This is your chance to shine and show everyone your talents.

You can sing, dance, act, play an instrument, or even do magic tricks!

Details
- Date: Friday, December 20th
- Time: 5:00 p.m. – 8:00 p.m.
- Place: School Auditorium

Tickets
- Students: $3.00
- Parents: $5.00
- Available: At the School Office
- Bring your loved ones to the show!

Important Information
- 1st floor: Snacks and drinks for purchase at the cafeteria
- 2nd floor: School office
- 3rd floor: School auditorium
- Make sure to come early, and grab a seat as soon as you arrive!

For More Information
- Contact: Ms. Gibson (School Manager)
- Phone: (132) 897-9237

Reading

32. What time does the talent show finish?

    (A) 5:00 pm
    (B) 7:00 pm
    (C) 8:00 pm

33. What does the sign suggest?

    (A) Bring your own food for the talent show
    (B) Come early and find a seat once you arrive
    (C) Do not come early, come right on time

34. Where can someone buy a ticket?

    (A) Online
    (B) In class
    (C) At the school office

35. How much cheaper is the student ticket than the adult ticket?

    (A) $2.00
    (B) $3.00
    (C) $5.00

Reading

Read the letter. Answer questions 36 and 37.

Hi Jayden,

I hope you're having a great week. I just got back from my family vacation in England and I had so much fun! It was so interesting to see Big Ben and the Tower Bridge. It was wonderful at night when all the lights came on, and so many people were taking photos. I also tried many different foods, and they all tasted great! But I think my favorite was fish and chips. It's my third time traveling abroad, and out of France, Spain, and England, I think I liked England the best. However, there were many rainy days, so I had to take an umbrella with me everywhere.

I know you're taking a family trip to England next month, so how about meeting up after school tomorrow so that I can tell you all about the things I did there?

From,
Tommy

36. What did Tommy like about England?

    (A)   He liked the beautiful landscape.

    (B)   He thought the people in England were friendly.

    (C)   He saw fascinating landmarks.

37. Why are Tommy and Jayden meeting up after school?

    (A)   Jayden will show the photos he took in England.

    (B)   Tommy will tell Jayden about his trip.

    (C)   Tommy will ask questions to Jayden about his trip.

Reading

Read the e-mail. Answer questions 38 and 39.

To: Coach Aaron
From: Paul
Subject: Basketball Practice

Dear Coach Aaron,
I hope you're having a great day. I wanted to ask if it's possible to reschedule our Tuesday basketball practice. My history exam got rescheduled, and unfortunately, it's at the same time as our practice session. As the basketball tournament is on Sunday, I don't want to miss out on training. I am free the day before the tournament, so please let me know if you could reschedule our practice session.
Thank you so much!

Sincerely,
Paul

38. Why can't Paul go to his basketball practice?

  (A) He can't go to school.
  (B) He needs to go to the basketball tournament.
  (C) He needs to take his history exam.

39. On what day will Coach Aaron probably reschedule Paul's training?

  (A) Tuesday
  (B) Saturday
  (C) Sunday

You finished the reading test.

Listening

Part 1 Actual Test 1 #01~08

Listen to the words. Look at the pictures.
Fill in the correct circles on your answer sheet.

Let's do an example.

1.

(A)

(B)

(C)

The answer is "A". Fill in "A" on your answer sheet.

Now, you do it.

2.

(A)

(B)

(C)

Listening

3.

(A)

(B)

(C)

4.

(A)

(B)

(C)

5.

(A)

(B)

(C)

Listening

6.

(A)　　　　　　　　　(B)　　　　　　　　　(C)

7.

(A)　　　　　　　　　(B)　　　　　　　　　(C)

8.

(A)　　　　　　　　　(B)　　　　　　　　　(C)

Listening

 # Listening

Part 2 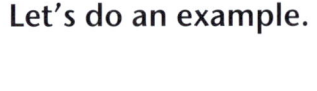 Actual Test 1 #09~18

Fill in the correct circles on your answer sheet.

Let's do an example.

9.

(A)

(B)

(C)

The answer is "B". Fill in "B" on your answer sheet.

Now, you do it.

10.

(A)

(B)

(C)

Listening

11.

(A)　　　　　　　　(B)　　　　　　　　(C)

12.

(A)　　　　　　　　(B)　　　　　　　　(C)

13.

(A)　　　　　　　　(B)　　　　　　　　(C)

Listening

14.

(A)　　　　　　　(B)　　　　　　　(C)

15.

(A)　　　　　　　(B)　　　　　　　(C)

16.

(A)　　　　　　　(B)　　　　　　　(C)

Listening

17.

(A)　　　　　　　　　(B)　　　　　　　　　(C)

18.

(A)　　　　　　　　　(B)　　　　　　　　　(C)

Listening

Part 3 Actual Test 1 #19~28

Fill in the correct circles on your answer sheet.

---

19. Look at your answer sheet. Listen to a conversation. Which conversation sounds correct?

Let's do an example.

The answer is "B". Fill in "B" on your answer sheet.

Now, you do it.

20.

21.

22.

23.

24.

25.

26.

27.

28.

38 Ace the TOEFL Primary Step 1

Listening

# Listening

Part 4 Actual Test 1 #29~35

Listen to a conversation and answer the question.
Fill in the correct circle on your answer sheet.

Let's do an example.

29. What drink will the boy get?

   (A)   A lemonade
   (B)   An apple smoothie
   (C)   An orange juice

The answer is "B". Fill in "B" on your answer sheet.

Now, you do it.

---

30. What did the girl NOT do at Girl Scout camp?

   (A)   Canoeing
   (B)   Horse riding
   (C)   Kayaking

31. Where will the girl sell her cake and muffins?

   (A)   At the bakery
   (B)   At the bake sale
   (C)   At the wholesale

32. What does the girl agree to do?

   (A)   Find her watch in the closet
   (B)   Clean out her closet
   (C)   Check again when finding something

40 Ace the TOEFL Primary Step 1

Listening

33. What will Daisy do after school?

    (A)   Go to Arthur's house

    (B)   Borrow a tennis racket

    (C)   Go and play tennis

34. What does Violet <u>NOT</u> need help with?

    (A)   Heating the oven

    (B)   Using a measuring scale

    (C)   Getting the measurements right

35. What will Sean do next?

    (A)   He will go to James's house and ask if he wants to go camping.

    (B)   He will call James to see if he has any plans for the weekend.

    (C)   He will go and buy marshmallows.

Listening

Part 5   Actual Test 1 #36~41

Listen and answer the question.
Fill in the correct circle on your answer sheet.

   Let's do an example.

36. What should the students bring to the speech?

   (A)   A camera
   (B)   A notebook
   (C)   A textbook

The answer is "B". Fill in "B" on your answer sheet.

Now, you do it.

---

37. Why did Shelby call?

   (A)   To ask Mrs. Harrington if she can pick her up
   (B)   To tell Mrs. Harrington that Elly left her things at her place
   (C)   To explain to Mrs. Harrington that Elly needs to practice tennis

38. Why did Olivia call?

   (A)   To tell Julie that she took a test today
   (B)   To tell Julie that she needs to make a speech about the poles
   (C)   To see if she needs help catching up

39. Why did Sara call?

   (A)   To tell Kate that she took the dogs for a walk
   (B)   To ask if Kate likes ice cream
   (C)   To see if Kate wants to go to the park

42 Ace the TOEFL Primary Step 1

Listening

40. Why did dad call?

(A) To ask if David can look after his sister
(B) To ask if David is going to be late
(C) To tell David to get home as soon as possible

41. What did the boy leave behind?

(A) His gym bag
(B) His baseball bat
(C) His lunch

You finished the listening test.

Actual Test 02

Reading

Part 1

Look at the picture. Read the words. Which words go with the picture?
Fill in the correct circles on your answer sheet.

Let's do two example questions.

1.

(A) The family is eating lunch.
(B) The family is making dinner.
(C) The family is eating dinner.

The answer is "C." Fill in "C" on your answer sheet.

2.

(A) Narrow
(B) Wide
(C) Broad

The answer is "A." Fill in "A" on your answer sheet.

Reading

3.

(A) Worm
(B) Ant
(C) Ladybug

4.

(A) Square
(B) Triangle
(C) Rectangle

Reading

5.

(A) Push
(B) Pull
(C) Drag

6.

(A) Lizard
(B) Caterpillar
(C) Crocodile

Reading

7.

(A) Dirty
(B) Clean
(C) Dark

8.

(A) Above
(B) Under
(C) On

Reading

9.

(A) Smaller
(B) Same
(C) Taller

10.

(A) Next to
(B) On
(C) In

Reading

11.

- (A) Driver
- (B) Detective
- (C) Dentist

12.

- (A) Catch
- (B) Throw
- (C) Kick

Reading

13.

(A) The cat is sitting next to the sofa.
(B) The dog is sitting on the sofa.
(C) The dog is sitting next to the sofa.

14.

(A) Lina's dad is tying his shoelace.
(B) Lina's dad is tying Lina's shoelace.
(C) Lina is trying to tie her shoelace.

Reading

15.

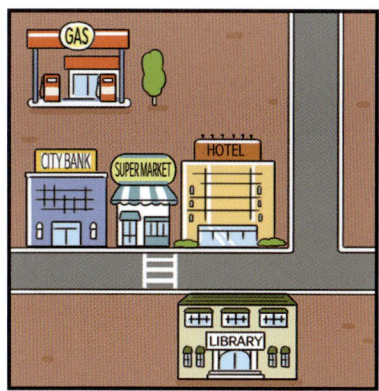

(A) The City Bank is next to the Hotel.
(B) The Hotel is across from the Library.
(C) The Library is behind the Gas Station.

16.

(A) The birds are sitting on branches.
(B) The birds are flying in the sky.
(C) The birds are making a nest.

Reading

17.

(A) The girl is selling fruits and vegetables.

(B) The man is cooking fruits and vegetables.

(C) The girl is buying fruits and vegetables.

Reading

Reading

Part 2

Read and find the answer.
Fill in the correct circles on your answer sheet.

Let's do an example.

18. He is trying to drink milk. He needs this to pour his milk. It is usually in the kitchen.

    What is it?

    (A) A dish
    (B) A spoon
    (C) A cup

    The answer is <u>a cup</u>. Fill in "C" on your answer sheet.

---

19. It eats different types of plants and vegetables. It is small, furry, and has long ears. It can run fast and hop around.

    What is it?

    (A) A mouse
    (B) A fox
    (C) A rabbit

20. People can travel long distances in these. They are long and have many seats. They run on tracks and can carry many people.

    What is it?

    (A) A plane
    (B) A bus
    (C) A train

56 Ace the TOEFL Primary Step 1

Reading

21. He is holding a rectangular-shaped object to his ear. He is talking to someone and looks happy.

    He is _____.

    (A) reading a book
    (B) on the phone
    (C) watching a movie

22. She is using brushes. She dips the brushes in different paints. The painting shows a cute dog.

    She is _____.

    (A) writing
    (B) drawing
    (C) cutting

23. People need this to protect their skin from the sun. It can come in different types, such as lotion or spray.

    What is it?

    (A) Sunglasses
    (B) Sunscreen
    (C) Sunlight

24. You don't know the meaning of a word. You try to ask your teacher, but she is busy. You look for a dictionary.

    You will _____ the meaning of the word.

    (A) pick out
    (B) show off
    (C) look up

Reading

25. A girl is trying to solve a math problem. Although she is having a hard time, she is still trying.

    The girl is not _____.

    (A) picking up
    (B) turning down
    (C) giving up

26. People put food in this to keep it cold and fresh. It also helps prevent food from getting spoiled. There is also a section to freeze things like ice cream.

    What is it?

    (A) An oven
    (B) A refrigerator
    (C) A dishwasher

27. You are walking down a street. You recognize someone you know. You start to wave to this person.

    You have _____ someone you know.

    (A) run into
    (B) turned into
    (C) looked into

Reading

Reading

Part 3

Fill in the correct circles on your answer sheet.

Read the after-school schedule 28 to 31.

Bella's After-School Schedule

	Mondays	Tuesdays	Wednesdays	Thursdays	Fridays
3:00 p.m.	Science Club	Tennis Club - Practicing for the tournament	Drama Club - At school	Homework	Play time
5:00 p.m.	Cleaning - Helping mom do the dishes	Dinner	Play time	Book Club - At the library	Play time
7:00 p.m.	Dinner	Homework	Dinner	Dance Club	Dinner - Dinner with grandparents
8:00 p.m.	Family time - Scrabble & board games	Bedtime	Bath time	Dinner	Family time

Reading

28. What club does Bella go to on Wednesdays?

    (A)   Tennis Club
    (B)   Book Club
    (C)   Drama Club

29. At what time does Bella eat dinner on Fridays?

    (A)   5:00 p.m.
    (B)   7:00 p.m.
    (C)   8:00 p.m.

30. When does Bella have two sessions of play time?

    (A)   On Mondays
    (B)   On Wednesdays
    (C)   On Fridays

31. What does Bella do at 7:00 p.m. on Tuesdays?

    (A)   Do homework
    (B)   Eat dinner
    (C)   Go to bed

Reading

Read the invitation. Answer questions 32 to 35.

South Westwick Graduation Party

South Westwick teachers invite all of the graduating students to have fun and excitement while making even more special memories.

We are all so proud of our hard-working and amazing students.

We want to celebrate your friendships and the wonderful memories you have made with one another.

Come and celebrate the end of your elementary school years!

Graduation Party Schedule

Face Painting	Library: 1st Floor	2:00 PM - 3:30 PM
Photo Booth	Gymnasium: 2nd Floor	All Day
Award Ceremony	Auditorium: 3rd Floor	4:00 PM – 5:00 PM
Balloon Burst	Gymnasium: 2nd Floor	5:00 PM – 5:30 PM
Dance Party	Auditorium: 3rd Floor	5:30 PM – 7:00 PM

All family members are invited to this party, so please be encouraged to attend and celebrate this special occasion.

Party food will include drinks and delicious cakes and cookies at the gymnasium.

Reading

32. Which activity has no time schedule?

    (A) Photo Booth
    (B) Award Ceremony
    (C) Dance Party

33. Where will the award be announced?

    (A) At the gymnasium
    (B) In the parking lot
    (C) In the auditorium

34. Where can someone get drinks?

    (A) On the 1st Floor
    (B) On the 2nd Floor
    (C) On the 3rd Floor

35. Why is South Westwick School having a graduation party?

    (A) To congratulate students going to high school
    (B) To celebrate students winning a competition
    (C) To praise students for their efforts

Reading

Read the e-mail. Answer questions 36 and 37.

To: Lina
From: Jordan
Subject: This weekend plans

Dear Lina,

I wanted to congratulate you on your outstanding performance at the piano concert last week. Your talent is truly impressive, and I wish you continued success in your future performances!
As a fun break, I am wondering if you would like to go ice skating with me and Chris this weekend. I heard that the new ice rink is really big, and there is even a snow festival happening. In fact, we can even make a snowman and play ice hockey.
We plan to leave at 10:00 a.m. and return around 7:00 p.m. If you can join us, let's meet in front of the school at 9:30 a.m. Let me know if you can come!

From,
Jordan

---

36. Why did Jordan write a letter to Lina?

    (A) To ask if he can borrow her skates

    (B) To ask if she can go ice skating this week

    (C) To ask if she can play ice hockey

37. What time will they get back home?

    (A) Approximately 10:00 a.m.

    (B) About 9:30 a.m.

    (C) Roughly 7:00 p.m.

Reading

Read the letter. Answer questions 38 and 39.

Dear Mrs. Williams,

Hello, this is Daisy. I wanted to tell you how helpful your speech about animal hibernation was. It was very interesting to know how animals eat enormous amounts of food to store fat before entering a deep sleep. It was also fascinating to know that their body temperature drops and their rate of breathing slows down.

I can't wait to sign up for more of your speeches! In fact, I heard from my dad that there is a speech about dinosaurs coming up next month. I'll make sure to study about them in detail before attending. Thank you again for your fantastic speech!

Sincerely,
Daisy

38. What does NOT happen when animals hibernate?

  (A) Their body temperature drops.
  (B) Their rate of breathing slows down.
  (C) They eat enormous amounts of food.

39. What will Daisy do before signing up for the next speech?

  (A) Write a speech about hibernation.
  (B) Watch a video about animals entering deep sleep.
  (C) Study about ancient creatures.

You finished the reading test.

 # Listening

Part 1   Actual Test 2 #01~08

Listen to the words. Look at the pictures.
Fill in the correct circles on your answer sheet.

Let's do an example.

1.

(A)   (B)   (C)

The answer is "B". Fill in "B" on your answer sheet.

Now, you do it.

2.

(A)   (B)   (C)

66 Ace the TOEFL Primary Step 1

Listening

3.

(A)   (B)   (C)

4.

(A)   (B)   (C)

5.

(A)   (B)   (C)

Listening

6.

(A)

(B)

(C)

7.

(A)

(B)

(C)

8.

(A)

(B)

(C)

68 Ace the TOEFL Primary Step 1

Listening

 # Listening

Part 2 Actual Test 2 #09~19

Fill in the correct circles on your answer sheet.

Let's do an example.

9.

(A)　　　　　　　　　(B)　　　　　　　　　(C)

The answer is "C". Fill in "C" on your answer sheet.

Now, you do it.

10.

(A)　　　　　　　　　(B)　　　　　　　　　(C)

Listening

11.

(A)   (B)   (C)

12.

(A)   (B)   (C)

13.

(A)   (B)   (C)

Listening

14.

(A) (B) (C)

15.

(A) (B) (C)

16.

(A) (B) (C)

Listening

17.

 (A)  (B)  (C)

18.

 (A)  (B)  (C)

19.

 (A) (B)  (C)

Listening

Part 3 Actual Test 2 #20~26

Fill in the correct circles on your answer sheet.

Look at your answer sheet. Listen to a conversation. Which conversation sounds correct?

Let's do an example.

20.

The answer is "B". Fill in "B" on your answer sheet.

Now, you do it.

21.

22.

23.

24.

25.

26.

Go On

74 Ace the TOEFL Primary Step 1

Listening

Listening

Part 4   Actual Test 2 #27~33

Listen to a conversation and answer the question.
Fill in the correct circle on your answer sheet.

Let's do an example.

27. Where will the girl go next?

    (A)   Go and play dodgeball
    (B)   Help the boy find his glasses
    (C)   Go to the gym

The answer is "C". Fill in "C" on your answer sheet.

Now, you do it.

---

28. What will the girl do next?

    (A)   Try her best to play the violin.
    (B)   Take violin lessons for three months.
    (C)   Put in effort to learn the piano.

29. What will the woman do next?

    (A)   Glue the paper flowers.
    (B)   Swing by the store and get the cake.
    (C)   Help Ellie finish her present.

30. What will the boy do next?

    (A)   Find his jacket
    (B)   Ask mom to find his blue sweater
    (C)   Go outside

Listening

31. What does the girl have to do first?

- (A) Finish her science project.
- (B) Finish doing the dishes.
- (C) Get ready to go to the movies.

32. What did the girl have trouble doing at first?

- (A) Teaching the boy how to surf.
- (B) Meeting a good teacher.
- (C) Standing on the surfboard.

33. What does the girl want to do?

- (A) She wants to buy the statue made from recycled goods.
- (B) She can't wait to go home and show the boy what she made.
- (C) She is eager to create something from reused goods.

Listening

Part 5 Actual Test 2 #34~41

Listen and answer the question.
Fill in the correct circle on your answer sheet.

Let's do an example.

34. What should students do first?

(A) Take part in a fire drill
(B) Have lunch
(C) Go out for recess

The answer is "B". Fill in "B" on your answer sheet.

Now, you do it.

---

35. Why did Agnes call?

(A) To ask if Aileen can pick up school supplies
(B) To ask if they can see each other at the mall
(C) To tell Aileen that she will be at her place

36. Why does Leo have to call James as soon as possible?

(A) To tell him how much he likes insects
(B) To ask if he wants to go to the Bug Science Fair
(C) To reserve tickets before they're all gone

37. Why did Lucy call dad?

(A) She needs to stay the night at Sally's place.
(B) She decided to do the group project with Sally.
(C) She asked her dad for a later pickup.

Listening

38. Why did Sophia call?

- (A) To praise Olivia for her performance
- (B) To invite Olivia to a performance
- (C) To ask Olivia for an invitation to the next performance

39. Where will the teachers be meeting?

- (A) At the school parking area
- (B) At the charity fund
- (C) At the Education for All charity center

40. Why did Mrs. Moore call Mrs. Jones?

- (A) To invite her to the assembly on Monday
- (B) To congratulate her for winning the Spelling Bee contest
- (C) To praise Aaron for winning the contest

41. Why did the guide make the announcement?

- (A) To explain where to go
- (B) To ask the class to leave
- (C) To tell the class to stay in a group

You finished the listening test.

Actual Test 03

Reading

Part 1

Look at the picture. Read the words. Which words go with the picture?
Fill in the correct circles on your answer sheet.

Let's do two example questions.

1.

(A) She is tired.
(B) She is sad.
(C) She is excited.

The answer is "A." Fill in "A" on your answer sheet.

2.

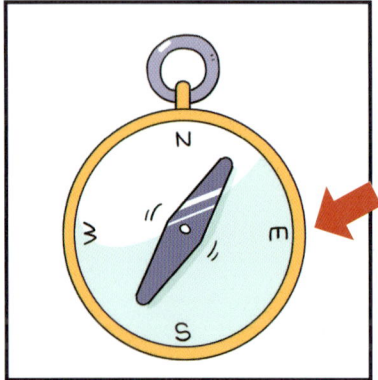

(A) East
(B) West
(C) South

The answer is "A." Fill in "A" on your answer sheet.

Reading

3.

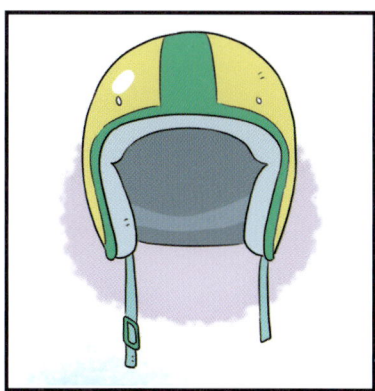

(A) Helmet
(B) Harp
(C) Hook

4.

(A) Mole
(B) Monkey
(C) Mouse

Reading

5.

- (A) Waves
- (B) Wind
- (C) Wish

6.

- (A) Shadow
- (B) Sand
- (C) Story

Reading

7.

(A) Dragon
(B) Deer
(C) Dragonfly

8.

(A) Thick
(B) Thin
(C) Heavy

Reading

9.

(A) Take out
(B) Put Into
(C) Put Over

10.

(A) Half
(B) Whole
(C) Quarter

Reading

11.

(A) Empty
(B) Full
(C) Disappear

12.

(A) The sun has set.
(B) The sun is coming up.
(C) The sun is shining.

Reading

13.

(A) The girl is reading under the tree.
(B) The girl is resting under the tree.
(C) The girl is running under the tree.

14.

(A) The boy is taking a photo.
(B) The boy is playing baseball.
(C) The boy is talking on the phone.

Reading

15.

(A) The girl is sitting on the bench.
(B) The girl is standing beside the bench.
(C) The girl is lying down on the bench.

16.

(A) Two girls are whistling.
(B) The girls are angry.
(C) One girl is whispering.

Reading

17.

- (A) They are playing table tennis.
- (B) They are playing tennis.
- (C) They are playing dodgeball.

18.

- (A) The van is going over the tunnel.
- (B) The van is going across the bridge.
- (C) The van is going through the tunnel.

Reading

Reading

Part 2

Read and find the answer.

Fill in the correct circles on your answer sheet.

Let's do an example.

19. People put this on to smell good. It is usually a liquid and has all different kinds of smells. Some of them smell sweet, fresh, and even flowery.

    What is it?

    (A) Sweat
    (B) Tears
    (C) Perfume

    The answer is perfume. Fill in "C" on your answer sheet.

---

20. These can help you do your schoolwork, watch videos, and communicate with people. They are portable and can be used almost anywhere.

    What are they?

    (A) Laptops
    (B) Keyboards
    (C) Radios

21. People put water in this. This helps to boil water quickly. People can use this to make hot chocolate and tea.

    What is it?

    (A) A tumbler
    (B) A flask
    (C) A kettle

Reading

22. Workers are gathered in a room. They are discussing plans for next year. Some give out ideas, while others write down notes.

    They are having a _____.

    (A) meeting
    (B) chore
    (C) puzzle

23. People use this when they stop reading. It is usually small and made of paper or plastic. It helps you keep your place in a book and can help you find where you left off.

    What is it?

    (A) A bookshelf
    (B) A bookmark
    (C) A booklet

24. These animals have four long, strong legs. They can run very fast, and people can ride on them.

    What is it?

    (A) A lion
    (B) A kangaroo
    (C) A horse

25. You are in a library. You finally found the books you need for your history project. You take them to the counter.

    You are _____ the books from the library.

    (A) checking out
    (B) picking out
    (C) working out

Reading

26. This helps people keep safe from bacteria and gets rid of germs. People can use it as a liquid or gel when they cannot wash their hands.

    What is it?

    (A) Hand sanitizer
    (B) A handkerchief
    (C) A pair of handcuffs

27. The boy is helping his mom in the kitchen. He goes out to the dining room with plates, forks, and knives. He takes them to the dining table.

    He is going to _____ the table for dinner.

    (A) show up
    (B) put off
    (C) set up

Reading

Reading

Part 3

Fill in the correct circles on your answer sheet.

Read the field trip schedule 28 to 31.

Westfield School Field Trip – First Semester: March

Time	Activity	Location
7:30 a.m.	**Depart From School** - At 8:00 a.m. - Students must arrive no later than quarter to eight.	School Parking Lot
9:00 a.m.	**Aquarium Tour** - Taking photos is not allowed.	City Aquarium
12:00 p.m.	**Lunch** - Please bring your own lunch.	City Aquarium: Cafeteria
1:00 p.m.	**Learning About Sea Animals** - All students must take notes. - There will be a test on what we learned next week.	City Aquarium: Main Hall
5:00 p.m.	**Back to School**	School Parking Lot - Arrival: Around 6:30 p.m.

Reading

28. What's the latest time the students should arrive at school?

    (A) 7:30 a.m.
    (B) 7:45 a.m.
    (C) 7:50 a.m.

29. What do students have to bring to the field trip?

    (A) A camera
    (B) Lunch from home
    (C) Extra clothes

30. Where can students eat lunch?

    (A) In the cafeteria
    (B) In the main hall
    (C) In the parking lot

31. What is the field trip schedule mainly about?

    (A) A list of sea animals that students can see.
    (B) How students will arrive at the aquarium.
    (C) What students will be doing on their school trip.

Reading

Read the sign. Answer questions 32 to 35.

West Field Elementary School Field Trip

When :
December 23rd Friday, 9:00 AM, School Parking Lot (Make sure to come at least thirty minutes early)
Where: Rolling Amusement Park
Wear: Comfortable clothes and sneakers to enjoy a range of activities

Bring :
Swimwear (if you want to swim), water, sunscreen, money for food and snacks

Activities
There will be many exciting activities for all!

Ice Skating Rink	Roller Coaster	Water Park	Live Concerts
Take the chance to enjoy skating on the ice	Thrilling rides for all (There will be an age limit for some rides)	Make sure that you bring your swimwear if you want to swim	Watch the exciting shows and meet many famous singers

Important Notice
- Permission Slips
  - Slips must be signed by a guardian and given back to your homeroom teacher
  - Must be returned by Wednesday, December 2nd
- Health Precautions
  - If your child has any health concerns, the school must be notified

Reading

32. At what time should students arrive at the school parking lot?

    (A) No later than 8:30 AM
    (B) At 9:00 AM
    (C) Around 9:30 AM

33. What do you have to bring if you want to enjoy the water park?

    (A) Sunscreen
    (B) Water
    (C) Swimwear

34. Why should students wear comfortable clothing?

    (A) There will be a running competition.
    (B) There will be many activities to enjoy.
    (C) The weather is going to be very hot.

35. What should parents do if their children have medical worries?

    (A) Ask the amusement park to sign a permission slip.
    (B) Let the school know about any health conditions.
    (C) Tell a homeroom teacher about how exciting this trip sounds.

Reading

Read the e-mail. Answer questions 36 and 37.

To: Stratford Art Gallery
From: Mrs. Granger
Subject: Questions about a school field trip

Dear Stratford Art Gallery Team,

I am a teacher at Martin International School and would love to take my students on a field trip to your art gallery. We are learning about Pablo Picasso at school, and I heard that there will be a special exhibition about the artist. Could you please let me know about the exhibition in detail? Also, we plan to take around 50 students, so would there be any space where they could eat lunch?
Thank you for your time. I look forward to hearing from you.

Best Regards,
Mrs. Granger

36. What does Mrs. Granger NOT ask about?

   (A) A place for students to take pictures.
   (B) Details about the exhibition.
   (C) A place for students to eat lunch.

37. Why does Mrs. Granger want to take her students to the art gallery?

   (A) She wants the students to learn how to paint.
   (B) She wants the students to learn more about an artist.
   (C) She wants the students to make an exhibition of Pablo Picasso.

Reading

Read the e-mail. Answer questions 38 and 39.

To: Students
From: Ms. Brown
Subject: Field Trip Reminder

Dear Students,

I hope you're looking forward to the upcoming field trip to New Forest next week. It will be an exciting event for all of you and a great opportunity to draw the surroundings.

As a reminder, you must not forget the following supplies that you'll need. Please make sure to bring your pencils, erasers and colored pencils. We will be drawing landscapes, so having many colored pencils will help make your drawing more colorful. Also, you must bring a lunch box and something to drink.
I look forward to seeing all of you on Monday!

From,
Ms. Brown

---

38. Why did Ms. Brown send a letter to her students?

    (A) To remind the class to come early to school
    (B) To remind them to hand in their drawing on Monday
    (C) To remind the class to bring their art supplies

39. What will the students be drawing?

    (A) Trees and flowers
    (B) Friends
    (C) Colored pencils

You finished the reading test.

# Listening

Part 1   Actual Test 3 #01~07

Listen to the words. Look at the pictures.
Fill in the correct circles on your answer sheet.

Let's do an example.

1.

(A)　　　　　　　　(B)　　　　　　　　(C)

The answer is "A". Fill in "A" on your answer sheet.

Now, you do it.

2.

(A)　　　　　　　　(B)　　　　　　　　(C)

Listening

3.

(A)

(B)

(C)

4.

(A)

(B)

(C)

5.

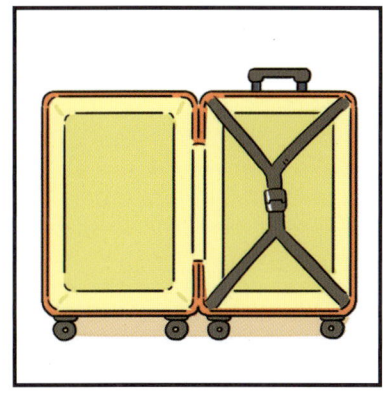
(A)

(B)

(C)

Listening

6.

(A)　　　　　　　　(B)　　　　　　　　(C)

7.

(A)　　　　　　　　(B)　　　　　　　　(C)

Listening

Listening

Part 2 Actual Test 3 #08~17

Fill in the correct circles on your answer sheet.

Let's do an example.

8.

(A) (B) (C)

The answer is "A". Fill in "A" on your answer sheet.

Now, you do it.

9.

(A) (B) (C)

106 Ace the TOEFL Primary Step 1

Listening

10.

(A) (B) (C)

11.

(A) (B) (C)

12.

(A) (B) (C)

Listening

13.

(A)   (B)   (C)

14.

(A)   (B)   (C)

15.

(A)   (B)   (C)

Listening

16.

(A)   (B)   (C)

17.

(A)   (B)   (C)

Listening

Part 3 Actual Test 3 #18~24

Fill in the correct circles on your answer sheet.

18.
Look at your answer sheet. Listen to a conversation. Which conversation sounds correct?

Let's do an example.

The answer is "B". Fill in "B" on your answer sheet.

Now, you do it.

19.

20.

21.

22.

23.

24.

Go On

Listening

Listening

Part 4 Actual Test 3 #25~33

Listen to a conversation and answer the question.
Fill in the correct circle on your answer sheet.

Let's do an example.

25. When will the girl have a sleepover?

   (A) Friday
   (B) This weekend
   (C) Next weekend

The answer is "C". Fill in "C" on your answer sheet.

Now, you do it.

---

26. What subject is the boy doing a project for?

   (A) Science
   (B) Social studies
   (C) Math

27. What does Coach Martin tell Alex to do?

   (A) To go home and get his baseball shirt
   (B) Be out in the baseball field as soon as he can
   (C) Borrow a baseball shirt from his friends

28. What is NOT a benefit of chocolate?

   (A) It can improve heart health.
   (B) It can bring about cavities.
   (C) It can make us feel better.

Listening

29. Why did Mr. Brown call Kevin?

    (A)   To tell him that the soccer tournament has been rescheduled.

    (B)   To tell him that his dad told him about the snowfall.

    (C)   To ask if he can make practice on Saturday.

30. What did the students see with a telescope?

    (A)   Jupiter

    (B)   Mars

    (C)   A magnifying glass

31. How are the students getting to school?

    (A)   On foot

    (B)   By taking the bus

    (C)   By taking the subway

32. Why did the mother and son have to wait so long in the boarding area?

    (A)   They had to have a medical check.

    (B)   The plane was having an engine check.

    (C)   They were waiting for their food to come.

33. Where will the students go next?

    (A)   The public library

    (B)   The school library

    (C)   The boy's home

Listening

Part 5 Actual Test 3 #34~41

Listen and answer the question.
Fill in the correct circle on your answer sheet.

Let's do an example.

34. Why did mom call Daisy?

   (A) To see if she needs her packed lunch
   (B) To tell her to call before going to the department store
   (C) To see if she needs anything from the department store

The answer is "A". Fill in "A" on your answer sheet.

Now, you do it.

---

35. Why did Julie call?

   (A) To tell her how excited Sally is for the sleepover
   (B) To see if there is anything more she can do
   (C) To invite Sally to her sleepover

36. What did Coach Miller ask Jake to do?

   (A) Help Kevin get to know his teammates
   (B) Introduce Kevin to a new coach
   (C) Congratulate Kevin for being the team captain

37. What did Tom call about?

   (A) A graduation ceremony
   (B) A gratitude party
   (C) A thank you note

114 Ace the TOEFL Primary Step 1

Listening

38. Why did Mrs. Turner call?

    (A) To tell her to bring along something to wear in the rain
    (B) To tell her that she doesn't want to catch a cold
    (C) To tell her that the trip is cancelled because of the rain

39. What did mom call about?

    (A) To remind her to pick up her new violin today
    (B) To not forget to call her violin teacher and thank her
    (C) To tell her that her violin strings can be tuned in two weeks

40. Why did Brian from the electronic store call?

    (A) To ask for a refund
    (B) To share news about a free gift
    (C) To return a new laptop

41. Why did Meredith's dad call?

    (A) To call him when she gets home
    (B) To tell her the competition will be moved up
    (C) To call her swimming coach

You finished the listening test.

EXAMPLE

YES	NO	NO	NO	NO
Ⓐ Ⓑ ●	Ⓐ Ⓑ ⊘	Ⓐ Ⓑ ⊗	Ⓐ Ⓑ Ⓒ	Ⓐ Ⓑ Ⓒ

Print your name in your first language:

Test Center Name:

Form Code:

Test Date:

SCHOOL USE ONLY
Is Consent Form on file? ◯ Yes ◯ No

1. NAME
Print your name. Using one box for each letter, first print your Given (first) name, then your Family (last) name. Below each box, use a No. 2 pencil and fill in the circle matching the same letter.

GIVEN (FIRST) NAME — FAMILY (LAST) NAME

2. STUDENT NUMBER
Start here

3. DATE OF BIRTH
Month / Day / Year

Jan, Feb, Mar, Apr, May, Jun, Jul, Aug, Sep, Oct, Nov, Dec

4. GENDER
BOY ◯
GIRL ◯

5. COUNTRY CODE

6. LANGUAGE CODE

7. At my school I am in:
◯ Grade 1
◯ Grade 2
◯ Grade 3
◯ Grade 4
◯ Grade 5
◯ Grade 6
◯ Grade 7
◯ Grade 8
◯ Grade 9
◯ Other

8. I have studied English for:
◯ 1 year or less
◯ 2 years
◯ 3 years
◯ 4 years
◯ 5 years
◯ 6 years or more

9. What test(s) have you taken before?
◯ TOEFL Primary Step 1
◯ TOEFL Primary Step 2
◯ Both
◯ None

10. GROUP CODE
(if assigned)

11. CODE SETS (if assigned)
CODE SET 1 | CODE SET 2 | CODE SET 3

PAGE 1

Reading

#		#		#	
1.	Ⓐ Ⓑ Ⓒ	14.	Ⓐ Ⓑ Ⓒ	27.	Ⓐ Ⓑ Ⓒ
2.	Ⓐ Ⓑ Ⓒ	15.	Ⓐ Ⓑ Ⓒ	28.	Ⓐ Ⓑ Ⓒ
3.	Ⓐ Ⓑ Ⓒ	16.	Ⓐ Ⓑ Ⓒ	29.	Ⓐ Ⓑ Ⓒ
4.	Ⓐ Ⓑ Ⓒ	17.	Ⓐ Ⓑ Ⓒ	30.	Ⓐ Ⓑ Ⓒ
5.	Ⓐ Ⓑ Ⓒ	18.	Ⓐ Ⓑ Ⓒ	31.	Ⓐ Ⓑ Ⓒ
6.	Ⓐ Ⓑ Ⓒ	19.	Ⓐ Ⓑ Ⓒ	32.	Ⓐ Ⓑ Ⓒ
7.	Ⓐ Ⓑ Ⓒ	20.	Ⓐ Ⓑ Ⓒ	33.	Ⓐ Ⓑ Ⓒ
8.	Ⓐ Ⓑ Ⓒ	21.	Ⓐ Ⓑ Ⓒ	34.	Ⓐ Ⓑ Ⓒ
9.	Ⓐ Ⓑ Ⓒ	22.	Ⓐ Ⓑ Ⓒ	35.	Ⓐ Ⓑ Ⓒ
10.	Ⓐ Ⓑ Ⓒ	23.	Ⓐ Ⓑ Ⓒ	36.	Ⓐ Ⓑ Ⓒ
11.	Ⓐ Ⓑ Ⓒ	24.	Ⓐ Ⓑ Ⓒ	37.	Ⓐ Ⓑ Ⓒ
12.	Ⓐ Ⓑ Ⓒ	25.	Ⓐ Ⓑ Ⓒ	38.	Ⓐ Ⓑ Ⓒ
13.	Ⓐ Ⓑ Ⓒ	26.	Ⓐ Ⓑ Ⓒ	39.	Ⓐ Ⓑ Ⓒ

Listening

#		#		#	
1.	Ⓐ Ⓑ Ⓒ	15.	Ⓐ Ⓑ Ⓒ	29.	Ⓐ Ⓑ Ⓒ
2.	Ⓐ Ⓑ Ⓒ	16.	Ⓐ Ⓑ Ⓒ	30.	Ⓐ Ⓑ Ⓒ
3.	Ⓐ Ⓑ Ⓒ	17.	Ⓐ Ⓑ Ⓒ	31.	Ⓐ Ⓑ Ⓒ
4.	Ⓐ Ⓑ Ⓒ	18.	Ⓐ Ⓑ Ⓒ	32.	Ⓐ Ⓑ Ⓒ
5.	Ⓐ Ⓑ Ⓒ	19.	Ⓐ Ⓑ Ⓒ	33.	Ⓐ Ⓑ Ⓒ
6.	Ⓐ Ⓑ Ⓒ	20.	Ⓐ Ⓑ Ⓒ	34.	Ⓐ Ⓑ Ⓒ
7.	Ⓐ Ⓑ Ⓒ	21.	Ⓐ Ⓑ Ⓒ	35.	Ⓐ Ⓑ Ⓒ
8.	Ⓐ Ⓑ Ⓒ	22.	Ⓐ Ⓑ Ⓒ	36.	Ⓐ Ⓑ Ⓒ
9.	Ⓐ Ⓑ Ⓒ	23.	Ⓐ Ⓑ Ⓒ	37.	Ⓐ Ⓑ Ⓒ
10.	Ⓐ Ⓑ Ⓒ	24.	Ⓐ Ⓑ Ⓒ	38.	Ⓐ Ⓑ Ⓒ
11.	Ⓐ Ⓑ Ⓒ	25.	Ⓐ Ⓑ Ⓒ	39.	Ⓐ Ⓑ Ⓒ
12.	Ⓐ Ⓑ Ⓒ	26.	Ⓐ Ⓑ Ⓒ	40.	Ⓐ Ⓑ Ⓒ
13.	Ⓐ Ⓑ Ⓒ	27.	Ⓐ Ⓑ Ⓒ	41.	Ⓐ Ⓑ Ⓒ
14.	Ⓐ Ⓑ Ⓒ	28.	Ⓐ Ⓑ Ⓒ		

EXAMPLE

YES	NO	NO	NO	NO
Ⓐ Ⓑ ●	Ⓐ Ⓑ ✓	Ⓐ Ⓑ ✗	Ⓐ ● Ⓒ	Ⓐ Ⓑ ⊘

Print your name in your first language:

Test Center Name:

Test Date:

Form Code:

SCHOOL USE ONLY
Is Consent Form on file? ○ Yes ○ No

1. NAME: Print your name. Using one box for each letter, first print your Given (first) name, then your Family (last) name. Below each box, use a No. 2 pencil and fill in the circle matching the same letter.

GIVEN (FIRST) NAME   FAMILY (LAST) NAME

2. STUDENT NUMBER — Start here

3. DATE OF BIRTH
Month | Day | Year
Jan, Feb, Mar, Apr, May, Jun, Jul, Aug, Sep, Oct, Nov, Dec

4. GENDER
BOY ○
GIRL ○

5. COUNTRY CODE

6. LANGUAGE CODE

7. At my school I am in:
○ Grade 1
○ Grade 2
○ Grade 3
○ Grade 4
○ Grade 5
○ Grade 6
○ Grade 7
○ Grade 8
○ Grade 9
○ Other

8. I have studied English for:
○ 1 year or less
○ 2 years
○ 3 years
○ 4 years
○ 5 years
○ 6 years or more

9. What test(s) have you taken before?
○ TOEFL Primary Step 1
○ TOEFL Primary Step 2
○ Both
○ None

10. GROUP CODE (if assigned)

11. CODE SETS (if assigned)
CODE SET 1 | CODE SET 2 | CODE SET 3

PAGE 1

Reading

1. (A) (B) (C)
2. (A) (B) (C)
3. (A) (B) (C)
4. (A) (B) (C)
5. (A) (B) (C)
6. (A) (B) (C)
7. (A) (B) (C)
8. (A) (B) (C)
9. (A) (B) (C)
10. (A) (B) (C)
11. (A) (B) (C)
12. (A) (B) (C)
13. (A) (B) (C)
14. (A) (B) (C)
15. (A) (B) (C)
16. (A) (B) (C)
17. (A) (B) (C)
18. (A) (B) (C)
19. (A) (B) (C)
20. (A) (B) (C)
21. (A) (B) (C)
22. (A) (B) (C)
23. (A) (B) (C)
24. (A) (B) (C)
25. (A) (B) (C)
26. (A) (B) (C)
27. (A) (B) (C)
28. (A) (B) (C)
29. (A) (B) (C)
30. (A) (B) (C)
31. (A) (B) (C)
32. (A) (B) (C)
33. (A) (B) (C)
34. (A) (B) (C)
35. (A) (B) (C)
36. (A) (B) (C)
37. (A) (B) (C)
38. (A) (B) (C)
39. (A) (B) (C)

Listening

1. (A) (B) (C)
2. (A) (B) (C)
3. (A) (B) (C)
4. (A) (B) (C)
5. (A) (B) (C)
6. (A) (B) (C)
7. (A) (B) (C)
8. (A) (B) (C)
9. (A) (B) (C)
10. (A) (B) (C)
11. (A) (B) (C)
12. (A) (B) (C)
13. (A) (B) (C)
14. (A) (B) (C)
15. (A) (B) (C)
16. (A) (B) (C)
17. (A) (B) (C)
18. (A) (B) (C)
19. (A) (B) (C)
20. (A) (B) (C)
21. (A) (B) (C)
22. (A) (B) (C)
23. (A) (B) (C)
24. (A) (B) (C)
25. (A) (B) (C)
26. (A) (B) (C)
27. (A) (B) (C)
28. (A) (B) (C)
29. (A) (B) (C)
30. (A) (B) (C)
31. (A) (B) (C)
32. (A) (B) (C)
33. (A) (B) (C)
34. (A) (B) (C)
35. (A) (B) (C)
36. (A) (B) (C)
37. (A) (B) (C)
38. (A) (B) (C)
39. (A) (B) (C)
40. (A) (B) (C)
41. (A) (B) (C)

EXAMPLE

YES	NO	NO	NO	NO
Ⓐ Ⓑ ●	Ⓐ Ⓑ ✓	Ⓐ Ⓑ ✗	Ⓐ Ⓑ Ⓒ	Ⓐ Ⓑ Ⓒ

Print your name in your first language:

Test Center Name:

Form Code:

Test Date:

SCHOOL USE ONLY
Is Consent Form on file? ◯ Yes ◯ No

1. NAME
Print your name. Using one box for each letter, first print your Given (first) name, then your Family (last) name. Below each box, use a No. 2 pencil and fill in the circle matching the same letter.

GIVEN (FIRST) NAME   FAMILY (LAST) NAME

2. STUDENT NUMBER — Start here

3. DATE OF BIRTH
Month / Day / Year
◯ Jan ◯ Feb ◯ Mar ◯ Apr ◯ May ◯ Jun ◯ Jul ◯ Aug ◯ Sep ◯ Oct ◯ Nov ◯ Dec

4. GENDER
BOY ◯
GIRL ◯

5. COUNTRY CODE

6. LANGUAGE CODE

7. At my school I am in:
◯ Grade 1
◯ Grade 2
◯ Grade 3
◯ Grade 4
◯ Grade 5
◯ Grade 6
◯ Grade 7
◯ Grade 8
◯ Grade 9
◯ Other

8. I have studied English for:
◯ 1 year or less
◯ 2 years
◯ 3 years
◯ 4 years
◯ 5 years
◯ 6 years or more

9. What test(s) have you taken before?
◯ TOEFL Primary Step 1
◯ TOEFL Primary Step 2
◯ Both
◯ None

10. GROUP CODE (if assigned)

11. CODE SETS (if assigned)
CODE SET 1 | CODE SET 2 | CODE SET 3

PAGE 1

채점자 사용하세요.

Reading

1. Ⓐ Ⓑ Ⓒ
2. Ⓐ Ⓑ Ⓒ
3. Ⓐ Ⓑ Ⓒ
4. Ⓐ Ⓑ Ⓒ
5. Ⓐ Ⓑ Ⓒ
6. Ⓐ Ⓑ Ⓒ
7. Ⓐ Ⓑ Ⓒ
8. Ⓐ Ⓑ Ⓒ
9. Ⓐ Ⓑ Ⓒ
10. Ⓐ Ⓑ Ⓒ
11. Ⓐ Ⓑ Ⓒ
12. Ⓐ Ⓑ Ⓒ
13. Ⓐ Ⓑ Ⓒ
14. Ⓐ Ⓑ Ⓒ
15. Ⓐ Ⓑ Ⓒ
16. Ⓐ Ⓑ Ⓒ
17. Ⓐ Ⓑ Ⓒ
18. Ⓐ Ⓑ Ⓒ
19. Ⓐ Ⓑ Ⓒ
20. Ⓐ Ⓑ Ⓒ
21. Ⓐ Ⓑ Ⓒ
22. Ⓐ Ⓑ Ⓒ
23. Ⓐ Ⓑ Ⓒ
24. Ⓐ Ⓑ Ⓒ
25. Ⓐ Ⓑ Ⓒ
26. Ⓐ Ⓑ Ⓒ
27. Ⓐ Ⓑ Ⓒ
28. Ⓐ Ⓑ Ⓒ
29. Ⓐ Ⓑ Ⓒ
30. Ⓐ Ⓑ Ⓒ
31. Ⓐ Ⓑ Ⓒ
32. Ⓐ Ⓑ Ⓒ
33. Ⓐ Ⓑ Ⓒ
34. Ⓐ Ⓑ Ⓒ
35. Ⓐ Ⓑ Ⓒ
36. Ⓐ Ⓑ Ⓒ
37. Ⓐ Ⓑ Ⓒ
38. Ⓐ Ⓑ Ⓒ
39. Ⓐ Ⓑ Ⓒ

Listening

1. Ⓐ Ⓑ Ⓒ
2. Ⓐ Ⓑ Ⓒ
3. Ⓐ Ⓑ Ⓒ
4. Ⓐ Ⓑ Ⓒ
5. Ⓐ Ⓑ Ⓒ
6. Ⓐ Ⓑ Ⓒ
7. Ⓐ Ⓑ Ⓒ
8. Ⓐ Ⓑ Ⓒ
9. Ⓐ Ⓑ Ⓒ
10. Ⓐ Ⓑ Ⓒ
11. Ⓐ Ⓑ Ⓒ
12. Ⓐ Ⓑ Ⓒ
13. Ⓐ Ⓑ Ⓒ
14. Ⓐ Ⓑ Ⓒ
15. Ⓐ Ⓑ Ⓒ
16. Ⓐ Ⓑ Ⓒ
17. Ⓐ Ⓑ Ⓒ
18. Ⓐ Ⓑ Ⓒ
19. Ⓐ Ⓑ Ⓒ
20. Ⓐ Ⓑ Ⓒ
21. Ⓐ Ⓑ Ⓒ
22. Ⓐ Ⓑ Ⓒ
23. Ⓐ Ⓑ Ⓒ
24. Ⓐ Ⓑ Ⓒ
25. Ⓐ Ⓑ Ⓒ
26. Ⓐ Ⓑ Ⓒ
27. Ⓐ Ⓑ Ⓒ
28. Ⓐ Ⓑ Ⓒ
29. Ⓐ Ⓑ Ⓒ
30. Ⓐ Ⓑ Ⓒ
31. Ⓐ Ⓑ Ⓒ
32. Ⓐ Ⓑ Ⓒ
33. Ⓐ Ⓑ Ⓒ
34. Ⓐ Ⓑ Ⓒ
35. Ⓐ Ⓑ Ⓒ
36. Ⓐ Ⓑ Ⓒ
37. Ⓐ Ⓑ Ⓒ
38. Ⓐ Ⓑ Ⓒ
39. Ⓐ Ⓑ Ⓒ
40. Ⓐ Ⓑ Ⓒ
41. Ⓐ Ⓑ Ⓒ

Memo

Ace the TOEFL Primary

Step 1 (Reading & Listening)

Answer Key

Ace the TOEFL Primary

Step 1 (Reading & Listening)

Answer Key

Actual Test 1

Reading

1	(C)	2	(B)	3	(C)	4	(B)
5	(C)	6	(B)	7	(A)	8	(B)
9	(A)	10	(B)	11	(B)	12	(B)
13	(B)	14	(A)	15	(B)	16	(C)
17	(C)	18	(C)	19	(A)	20	(B)
21	(A)	22	(B)	23	(A)	24	(B)
25	(A)	26	(C)	27	(B)	28	(C)
29	(A)	30	(B)	31	(C)	32	(B)
33	(B)	34	(C)	35	(A)	36	(C)
37	(B)	38	(C)	39	(B)		

Part 1.

1. (A) 그녀는 옷을 쇼핑하는 중이다.
   (B) 그녀는 음식을 먹는 중이다.
   (C) 그녀는 식료품을 쇼핑하는 중이다.

2. (A) 잡다
   (B) 치다
   (C) 던지다

3. (A) 코뿔소
   (B) 곰
   (C) 코끼리

4. (A) 빗
   (B) 거울
   (C) 가위

5. (A) 걷다
   (B) 달리다
   (C) 뛰어오르다

6. (A) 정원
   (B) 부엌
   (C) 침실

7. (A) 여행하다
   (B) 쉬다
   (C) 공부하다

8. (A) 굽다
   (B) 칠하다
   (C) 공부하다

9. (A) 무릎
   (B) 발목
   (C) 팔꿈치

10. (A) 금성
    (B) 지구
    (C) 화성

11. (A) 거대한
    (B) 작은
    (C) 큰

12. (A) 소녀는 이야기를 하고 있다.
    (B) 소녀는 잠을 자고 있다.
    (C) 소녀는 춤을 추고 있다.

13. (A) 나무는 두 명의 아이들 앞에 있다.
    (B) 나무는 두 명의 아이들 사이에 있다.
    (C) 나무는 두 명의 아이들 뒤에 있다.

14. (A) 1개의 자가 있다.
    (B) 2개의 계산기가 있다.
    (C) 5자루의 연필이 있다.

15. (A) 오른쪽에 있는 소녀는 왼쪽에 있는 소녀보다 더 긴 머리를 가지고 있다.
    (B) 왼쪽에 있는 소녀는 오른쪽에 있는 소녀보다 더 긴 머리를 가지고 있다.
    (C) 왼쪽에 있는 소녀는 오른쪽에 있는 소녀보다 짧은 머리를 가지고 있다.

16. (A) 그는 뜨거운 것을 먹고 있다.
    (B) 그는 신 것을 먹고 있다.
    (C) 그는 단 것을 먹고 있다.

17. (A) 소년은 나무를 심고 있다.
    (B) 소녀는 사과를 기르고 있다.
    (C) 소년은 사과를 따고 있다.

18. (A) 소녀는 잘 준비를 하고 있다.
    (B) 소녀는 그녀의 담요를 빨고 있다.
    (C) 소녀는 그녀의 이불을 개고 있다.

Part 2.

19. 당신은 이것 안에 공기를 불어넣을 수 있습니다. 그것은 주로 동그랗고 여러 색깔을 가지고 있으며 주로 파티에서 사용됩니다. 이것은 무엇일까요?

    (A) 풍선
    (B) 케이크
    (C) 호루라기

20. 이것은 길고 주로 노란색이나 초록색입니다. 당신이 이것의 껍질을 벗기고 한 입 베어 물면 그것은 부드럽고 단 맛이 납니다. 이것은 무엇일까요?

    (A) 코코넛
    (B) 바나나
    (C) 키위

21. 당신은 펜, 연필 그리고 지우개와 같은 문구 용품을 보관 할 때 꼭 필요한 것입니다. 이것은 당신이 필기구를 가지고 다닐 수 있게 도와줍니다. 이것은 무엇일까요?

    (A) 필통
    (B) 컴퓨터
    (C) 책상

22. 당신은 수학 수업 중에 있습니다. 당신은 문제를 풀기 위해서 계산기가 필요하지만 가지고 있지 않습니다. 당신은 당신의 친구에게 부탁을 해야 합니다.
    당신은 당신의 친구에게 계산기를 _____ 중이다.

    (A) 빌려주는
    (B) 빌리는
    (C) 보내는

23. 그는 선이 그어진 코트 위에 있습니다. 그는 라켓으로 공을 세게 쳤고, 공은 네트를 넘어갑니다.
    그는 _____.

    (A) 테니스를 치는 중이다.
    (B) 골프를 하는 중이다.
    (C) 하키를 하는 중이다.

24. 날씨가 추울 때, 사람들은 따뜻함을 유지하기 위해 이것들을 목 주위에 두릅니다. 이것들은 다양한 크기, 모양 그리고 색깔이 있습니다. 이것들은 무엇일까요?

    (A) 장갑
    (B) 스카프
    (C) 부츠

25. 그들은 다른 소리를 만들어 낼 수 있습니다. 그들은 다양한 모양과 크기를 가지고 있습니다. 사람들은 그것들로 음악을 만들 수 있습니다. 그들은 무엇일까요?

    (A) 악기
    (B) 양초
    (C) 그림

26. 날씨는 춥거나 덥지 않습니다. 많은 꽃들과 식물들이 자라나기 시작하고, 모든 것들이 새롭고 신선하게 느껴집니다.
    그것은 _____이다.

    (A) 여름
    (B) 가을
    (C) 봄

27. 당신은 과학 프로젝트에 관한 정보를 얻고 싶습니다. 당신은 많은 책이 있는 공간으로 가기로 결정합니다.
    당신은 _____을/를 갈 것이다.

    (A) 박물관
    (B) 도서관
    (C) 카페

Part 3.

[28-31] 아래를 읽고, 28–31번 질문에 답하세요.

날짜	층	활동	입장료
		우주과학박물관	
1/5	1F	태양계 체험 – 3D 행성 전시회 – 우주에 대해 배우기	$ 10.00
1/16	2F	로켓 만들기 – 풍선 로켓 만들기 – 파트너와 함께 활동하기	$ 15.00
1/21	2F	우주복 입어보기 – 실제 우주 비행사의 우주복	$ 25.00
1/25	3F	로켓 모델들 구경하기 – 사진 부스 – 우주복을 입고 사진 촬영하기	$ 20.00

28. 어떤 활동의 참가비가 가장 비싼가요?

    (A) 태양계 탐험하기
    (B) 로켓 만들기
    (C) 우주복 입어보기

29. 사람들은 언제 우주에 대해 배울 수 있습니까?

    (A) 1월 5일
    (B) 1월 16일
    (C) 1월 25일

30. 사람들은 우주복을 몇 층에서 입어 볼 수 있습니까?

    (A) 1층
    (B) 2층
    (C) 3층

31. 어떤 활동을 함께 협력해서 해야 합니까?

    (A) 로켓 모델 구경하기
    (B) 태양계 체험하기
    (C) 로켓 만들기

[32-35] 다음 글을 읽고, 정답을 고르시오.

모든 학생 여러분 주목해주세요!

올해의 탤런트 쇼를 발표하게 되어 우리는 매우 기쁩니다.
이 기회는 당신의 재능을 빛내고 모두에게 보여줄 수 있습니다.
당신은 노래, 춤, 연기, 악기 연주 또는 마술쇼를 할 수도 있습니다.

세부사항
날짜 : 12월 20일, 금요일
시간 : 오후 5시~8시
장소 : 학교 강당

티켓
학생 : 3달러
학부모 : 5달러
구매처 : 학교 사무실
당신이 사랑하는 사람을 초대하세요!

중요 참고 사항
1층 : 카페에서 간식과 음료 구매 가능
2층 : 학교 사무실
3층 : 학교 강당
일찍 도착해서, 자리를 잡으세요!

더 많은 정보를 원하시면 아래로 연락주세요.
연락처 : Gibson (학교 매니저)
핸드폰 : (132) 897-9237

32. 탤런트 쇼는 언제 끝나나요?
    (A) 오후 5시
    (B) 오후 7시
    (C) 오후 8시

33. 위 글에서 알 수 있는 내용은 무엇인가요?
    (A) 탤런트 쇼에서 먹을 음식은 직접 가져오기
    (B) 일찍 와서 자리 찾기
    (C) 일찍 오지 말고, 정각에 오기

34. 티켓은 어디서 살 수 있습니까?
    (A) 온라인
    (B) 교실
    (C) 학교 사무실

35. 학생 티켓은 어른 티켓보다 얼마나 저렴합니까?
    (A) 2달러
    (B) 3달러
    (C) 5달러

[36-37] 편지를 읽고, 36-37번 질문에 답하세요.

안녕, Jayden.

한 주 잘 보냈어? 나는 영국에서 보낸 가족 휴가를 끝내고 이제 막 돌아왔는데, 너무 재미있었어!
Big Ben과 Tower Bridge를 본 것은 매우 흥미로웠어. 저녁에 모든 불이 들어왔을 때 너무 아름다웠고, 많은 사람들이 사진을 찍었어. 또한 많은 음식을 시도해보았고, 그것들은 전부 맛있었어! 그러나 내가 생각하기에 가장 맛있었던 것은 피쉬앤칩스였어. 이번이 세 번째 해외여행인데 프랑스, 스페인, 영국 중에서 영국이 가장 좋았어. 그러나 비가 내리는 날이 많아. 그래서 나는 어디를 가든 우산을 써야 했어. 네가 다음달에 영국으로 가족 여행을 간다고 알고 있어. 그래서 내일 방과 후에 내가 그곳에서 했던 모든 것을 얘기해주고 싶은데 만나는 게 어때?

Tommy로부터

36. Tommy는 영국에 대해 무엇을 좋아했나요?
    (A) 그는 아름다운 풍경을 좋아했다.
    (B) 그는 영국에 사는 사람들이 친근하다고 생각했다.
    (C) 그는 인상적인 명소들을 보았다.

37. Tommy와 Jaden은 왜 방과 후에 만나나요?
    (A) Jayden은 그가 영국에서 찍은 사진을 보여줄 것이다.
    (B) Tommy는 Jayden 에게 그의 여행에 대해서 말해줄 것이다.
    (C) Tommy는 Jayden 에게 그의 여행에 대해서 질문을 할 것이다.

[38-39] 편지를 읽고, 38-39번 질문에 답하세요.

받는 사람: Aaron코치님께
보내는 사람: Paul
주제: 농구 연습

Aaron코치님께

안녕하세요. 코치님. 저는 화요일 농구 연습을 다른 요일로 변경이 가능한지 여쭤보고 싶어요. 역사 시험 일자가 변경되어 안타깝게도 우리의 연습 일정과 겹치게 되었어요. 농구 경기가 일요일이기에 저는 연습에 빠지고 싶지 않아요. 저는 경기 전날에 여유가 있으니 코치님께서 연습 일정을 변경하실 수 있는지 알려주세요.
감사합니다!

진심을 담아
Paul

38. Paul은 왜 농구 훈련에 갈 수 없나요?
    (A) 그는 학교에 갈 수 없다.
    (B) 그는 농구 시합에 참가해야 한다.
    (C) 그는 역사 시험을 봐야 한다.

39. Aaron코치는 Paul의 연습을 어떤 날로 다시 정할까요?

(A) 화요일
(B) 토요일
(C) 일요일

Listening

1 (A)	2 (C)	3 (C)	4 (B)
5 (A)	6 (B)	7 (C)	8 (A)
9 (B)	10 (C)	11 (B)	12 (A)
13 (C)	14 (B)	15 (C)	16 (B)
17 (A)	18 (A)	19 (B)	20 (A)
21 (C)	22 (B)	23 (B)	24 (B)
25 (C)	26 (A)	27 (C)	28 (B)
29 (B)	30 (B)	31 (B)	32 (C)
33 (C)	34 (B)	35 (B)	36 (B)
37 (B)	38 (C)	39 (C)	40 (A)
41 (A)			

Part 1.

1. She is getting a certificate.

그녀는 상장을 받는 중이다.

2. The brown dog is cleaner than the white dog.

갈색 개는 하얀색 개보다 더 깨끗하다.

3. They are hiding inside a closet.

그들은 옷장 안에 숨어 있는 중이다.

4. She is trying to catch the train.

그녀는 기차를 타려고 노력하는 중이다.

5. It's frosty outside.

바깥은 서리가 내렸다.

6. Her hair is tied.

그녀의 머리는 묶여 있다.

7. The lights are off.

불이 꺼져 있다.

8. He did NOT do the laundry.

그는 빨래를 하지 않았다.

Part 2.

9.
W: Listen to a girl.
G: Dad, I have a swimming competition this weekend. Can you help me practice? I really want to perform my best.
W: What did the girl ask her dad?

W: 소녀가 하는 얘기를 들어보세요.
G: 아빠 저는 이번 주말에 수영 시합이 있어요. 연습하는 것을 도와 주실 수 있을까요? 저는 최선을 다하고 싶어요.
W: 딸이 아빠에게 요청한 바는 무엇입니까?

10.
W: Listen to a mother.
W: Lina, can you call your grandmother and ask her if she can wait inside the bakery? I'm on my way now.
W: What did the mother tell her daughter to do?

W: 엄마가 하는 얘기를 들어보세요.
W: Lina, 할머니께 전화해서 빵집 안에서 기다리실 수 있는지 여쭤 봐줄래? 엄마는 지금 가는 중이야.
W: 엄마가 딸에게 무엇을 해달라고 하였습니까?

11.
W: Listen to an art teacher.
W: We're now going to color the pictures. If you didn't bring your coloring pencils, share with a friend next to you.
W: What did the teacher tell the students to do?

W: 미술 선생님이 하는 얘기를 들어보세요.
W: 우리는 이제 그림에 색을 칠할 거예요. 만약 색연필을 가져오지 않았다면 옆 친구와 같이 쓰도록 하세요.
W: 선생님은 학생들에게 무엇을 하라고 했습니까?

12.
W: Listen to a teacher.
M: Before we play basketball, we're going to stretch our muscles. Please stand in line and look at the teacher.
W: What did the teacher ask the students to do?

W: 선생님이 하는 얘기를 들어보세요.
M: 우리는 농구를 하기 전에 스트레칭 먼저 할 예정이예요. 선생 님을 보고 줄을 서세요.
W: 선생님은 학생들에게 무엇을 하라고 하였습니까?

13.
W: Listen to a mother.
W: Sally, thank you for helping me make dinner. Now please go and wash your hands before we start eating.
W: What did the mother tell her daughter to do?

W: 엄마가 하는 얘기를 들어보세요.
W: Sally, 저녁을 만드는 것을 도와주어 고맙구나. 이제 손을 씻고 와서 저녁을 먹자구나.
W: 엄마는 딸에게 무엇을 하라고 하였습니까?

14.
W: Listen to a mother.
W: Steve, could you turn the volume down? I have to talk to your grandfather, and it's too loud in here.
W: What did the mother ask her son to do?

W: 엄마가 하는 얘기를 들어보세요.
W: Steve, 소리를 낮춰줄 수 있겠니? 할아버지와 얘기를 나누어야 하는데 너무 시끄럽구나.
W: 엄마는 아들에게 무엇을 해달라고 부탁하였습니까?

15.
W: Listen to a boy.
B: Aaron, I know how much you like to play tennis, but the weather is too cold today. How about we stay in and play table tennis instead?
W: What did the boy suggest to his friend?

W: 소년이 하는 얘기를 들어보세요.
B: Aaron, 네가 얼마나 테니스 치는 것을 좋아하는지 알아. 그러나 오늘 밖의 날씨가 너무 추워. 오늘은 대신 탁구를 하는 것이 어떨까?
W: 소년은 그의 친구에게 무엇을 하자고 제안하였습니까?

16.
W: Listen to a girl.
G: Mom, can you pack my lunch tomorrow? Diane and I were going to eat at a restaurant, but I don't think we're going to have time.
W: What did the girl ask her mother to do?

W: 소녀가 하는 얘기를 들어보세요.
G: 엄마, 내일 점심을 싸 주실 수 있어요? Diane과 레스토랑에서 먹을 예정이었는데 그럴 시간이 없을 것 같아요.
W: 딸은 엄마에게 무엇을 해달라고 부탁하였습니까?

17.
W: Listen to a computer teacher.
M: Learning to use a keyboard can be difficult at first but when you get the hang of it, you can write much faster than writing with a pen. Now, please turn on your computers, everyone.
W: What did the teacher tell the students to do?

W: 컴퓨터 선생님이 하는 얘기를 들어보세요.
M: 키보드 사용법을 배우는 것은 처음에는 어려울 수 있지만, 익숙해지면 펜으로 쓰는 것보다 훨씬 더 빨리 쓸 수 있습니다. 이제 모두 컴퓨터를 켜세요.
W: 선생님은 학생들에게 무엇을 하라고 했습니까?

18.
W: Listen to a father.
M: Jordan, well done! You can now ride a bike without anyone's help! How about we get you your own bike now?
W: What did the father suggest to his son?

W: 아빠가 하는 얘기를 들어보세요.
M: Jordan, 잘했어! 이제 다른 사람의 도움없이 자전거를 탈 수 있네! 이제 네 자전거를 사러가는게 어떨까?
W: 아빠는 아들에게 무엇을 제안하였습니까?

Part 3.

19.
G: Which dress should I get?
(A) I can see well now.
(B) I loved the blue one.
(C) There are too many people.

G: 어떤 드레스를 사야 할까요?
(A) 나는 이제 잘 보여.
(B) 나는 파란색 드레스가 제일 좋았어.
(C) 너무 사람이 많아.

[20-22] Listen to a boy talking to his friend.
소년이 친구에게 하는 말을 들어보세요.

20.
B: Are your new running shoes comfortable?
(A) Yes, they're great for running.
(B) Of course, they help me go fast in the water.
(C) No, they don't match my skates.

B: 너의 새 운동화는 편하니?
(A) 응, 그 신발은 달리기 할 때 좋아.
(B) 물론이지, 이 신발은 내가 물속에서 빠르게 갈 수 있도록 도와줘.
(C) 아니, 그 신발은 내 스케이트와 어울리지 않아.

21.
B: Where did you get them?
(A) They aren't new.
(B) From the running tracks
(C) Online

B: 그거 어디서 구했어?

(A) 그것들은 새 것이 아니야.
(B) 운동장에서
(C) 온라인에서

22.
B: Can I try them on?

(A) Sure, I'll show you where you can find one.
(B) No problem, here you go.
(C) Of course, they're not my size.

B: 내가 신어봐도 될까?

(A) 물론이지. 내가 어디서 찾을 수 있는지 보여줄게.
(B) 그럼, 여기 있어.
(C) 물론, 그것들은 내 사이즈가 아니야.

[23-25] Listen to a mother talking to her son.
엄마가 아들에게 하는 얘기를 들어보세요.

23.
W: Are you ready to go to bed?

(A) I can't wait to see it.
(B) I don't know if I can fall asleep.
(C) I won't go tomorrow.

W: 너는 잠 잘 준비가 되었니?

(A) 나는 그것이 정말 기대 돼요.
(B) 나는 내가 잠에 들 수 있을 지 모르겠어요.
(C) 나는 내일 가지 않을 거예요.

24.
W: Are you excited for tomorrow?

(A) No, I am.
(B) Yes, very.
(C) Yes, yesterday was so much fun.

W: 너는 내일이 기대되니?

(A) 아니요. 기대돼요.
(B) 네, 정말 기대돼요.
(C) 네, 어제는 정말 재밌었어요.

25.
W: How about we turn the lights out?

(A) It's too bright anyway.
(B) I turned them on.
(C) They are already off.

W: 우리 불을 끄는 게 어때?

(A) 어차피 너무 밝아요.
(B) 내가 켰어요.
(C) 이미 꺼져있어요.

[26-28] Listen to a husband talking to his wife.
남편이 아내에게 하는 말을 들어보세요.

26.
M: What time are you picking up Sally?

(A) Something came up. Can you pick her up instead?
(B) It's too late. How about we order a meal?
(C) I know you're running late. Would you like Sally to pick you up?

M: Sally를 몇 시에 데리러 갈 거야?

(A) 일이 생겼어. 당신이 대신 데리러 갈 수 있어?
(B) 너무 늦었어. 식사를 주문하는게 어때?
(C) 당신이 늦는 거 알아. Sally 보고 데리러 가라고 할까?

27.
M: Sure, I'll go. What time do you want me to pick her up?

(A) Great! I'll tell her to come by herself.
(B) Thank you. I'll do it this time.
(C) Thanks! You need to go get her in an hour.

M: 물론이지, 내가 갈게. 몇 시에 데리러 갈까?

(A) 좋아! 그녀 혼자 오라고 할게.
(B) 고마워. 이번에는 내가 할게.
(C) 고마워. 1시간 후에 데리러 가면 돼.

28.
M: I'm driving back home with Sally. What are you thinking of having for dinner?

(A) Did you pick her up yet?
(B) How does pasta sound?
(C) I was thinking, why not?

M: Sally랑 같이 집으로 가고 있어.

(A) 아직도 그녀를 데리러 가지 않았어?
(B) 파스타 어때?
(C) 내 생각에는, 그럴까?

Part 4.

29.
W: Listen to a conversation between two students. Listen for the answer to this question.

G: I'm so thirsty, I need a drink.
B: How about we get a lemonade or an orange juice?
G: I was thinking of getting an apple smoothie.
B: Great choice; I'll get the same one.
W: What drink will the boy get?

W: 두 학생 사이의 대화를 듣고 질문에 답하세요.

G: 나는 목이 너무 말라. 마실 것이 필요해.

B: 레모네이드나 오렌지주스를 먹는 것은 어때?
G: 나는 사과 스무디를 마실까 생각 중이야.
B: 훌륭한 선택이다. 나도 같은 걸로 마실래.

W: 소년은 어떤 음료를 마시려고 하나요?

(A) 레모네이드
(B) 사과 스무디
(C) 오렌지 주스

30.
W: Listen to a conversation between a boy and a girl. Listen for the answer to this question.

B: Wow, Grace, look at your tan!
G: I just got back from Girl Scout camp. It was so much fun!
B: I'm sure it was. What did you do there?
G: Well, I couldn't go horse riding, but I went canoeing and even kayaking.
B: You must have had great fun!
G: I certainly did! How about you join the Boy Scouts next year?
W: What did the girl NOT do at Girl Scout camp?

W: 소년과 소녀 사이의 대화를 듣고 질문에 답하세요.

B: 와, Grace, 너 피부 탄거 봐!
G: 나는 걸스카우트 캠프에서 이제 막 돌아왔어. 너무 재밌었어!
B: 정말 그랬을 것 같아. 거기서 무엇을 했어?
G: 나는 승마는 못했지만, 카누와 카약을 탔어.
B: 정말 재밌었겠다!
G: 응! 너는 내년에 보이스카우트에 가입하는 것은 어때?

W: 소녀가 걸스카우트에서 하지 않은 활동은 무엇입니까?

(A) 카누 타기
(B) 말 타기
(C) 카약 타기

31.
W: Listen to a conversation between two students. Listen for the answer to this question.

B: What are you selling at the bake sale today?
G: I'm going to sell chocolate cake and muffins!
B: Wow! Did you bake that chocolate cake? It looks delicious!
G: Thank you. My grandma helped me bake it. She's a great cook.
B: I bet! How much is a piece?
G: I was thinking $2 for the chocolate cake and $1 for the muffins.
W: Where will the girl sell her cake and muffins?

W: 두 학생 사이의 대화를 듣고 질문에 답하세요.

B: 오늘 베이크 세일에서 무얼 팔거야?
G: 나는 초콜릿 케이크와 머핀을 팔 예정이야.
B: 와, 초콜릿 케이크는 네가 직접 구운 거니? 정말 맛있어 보인다!
G: 고마워. 할머니께서 굽는 것을 도와주셨어. 우리 할머니는 요리를 정말 잘하셔.
B: 그럴 것 같아! 한 조각에 얼마야?
G: 초콜릿 케이크는 조각 당 2달러이고, 머핀은 개 당 1달러로 생각하고 있어.

W: 소녀는 어디에서 초콜릿 케이크와 머핀을 판매하고 있습니까?

(A) 베이커리에서
(B) 베이크 세일에서
(C) 도매시장에서

32.
W: Listen to a conversation between a father and his daughter. Listen for the answer to this question.

G: I finally found my watch.
M: Where was it?
G: In the closet, underneath my purple blouse.
M: I thought you looked in the closet yesterday.
G: Sorry, dad, I did, but I think I didn't look hard enough.
M: It's OK, but be more careful next time.
G: OK, I'll make sure to look through it thoroughly.
W: What does the girl agree to do?

W: 아빠와 딸 사이의 대화를 듣고 질문에 답하세요.

G: 마침내 제 시계를 찾았어요.
M: 어디에 있었니?
G: 옷장 안에 있었어요. 제 보라색 블라우스 밑에요.
M: 네가 어제 옷장을 살펴본 줄 알았구나.
G: 죄송해요, 아빠. 찾아봤지만 충분히 보이지 않았나봐요.
M: 괜찮단다. 하지만 다음에는 잘 확인하렴.
G: 네, 자세하게 살펴볼게요.

W: 소녀가 하기로 동의한 것은 무엇입니까?

(A) 옷장에서 그녀의 시계를 찾기
(B) 그녀의 옷장을 청소하기
(C) 어떤 것을 찾을 때 다시 확인하기

33.
W: Listen to a conversation between two students at school. Listen for the answer to this question.

G: Arthur, do you want to play tennis with me after school?
B: Sure, Daisy! I was looking for a partner to play with.
G: I know, it's so hard to find a partner these days.
B: Tell me about it. When do you want to play?

G: How about we head over to the courts straight after school?
B: Could we swing by my place first? I left my tennis racket at home.
G: You can borrow mine; I have two more.
B: Thanks, that would be great.
W: What will Daisy do after school?

W: 학교에서 두 학생 사이의 대화를 듣고 질문에 답하세요.
G: Arthur, 방과 후에 나랑 같이 테니스를 치지 않을래?
B: 좋지 Daisy! 나도 같이 할 파트너를 찾고 있는 중이었어.
G: 그치, 요즘은 파트너 찾는 게 정말 힘들어.
B: 내말이. 언제 치러갈까?
G: 방과 후에 바로 코트로 가는 건 어때?
B: 우리 집에 먼저 잠깐 들를 수 있을까? 테니스 라켓을 집에 두고 왔어.
G: 내거 빌려도 돼. 나 여분이 두 개 더 있어.
B: 고마워. 그래주면 너무 좋을 것 같아.

W: 소녀가 하기로 동의한 것은 무엇입니까?

(A) Arthur의 집에 가기
(B) 테니스 라켓을 빌리기
(C) 테니스 치러 가기

34.
W: Listen to a conversation between a mother and her daughter. Listen for the answer to this question.
G: Mom, can you help me bake these chocolate chip cookies?
W: Sure, I can. What do you need help with?
G: I always have a hard time measuring the ingredients.
W: That can happen. All you need is a measuring scale.
G: Thank you! I know how to use one! Also, can you help me preheat the oven?
W: Of course, but instead of me doing it for you, how about I show you?
G: That's a great idea, mom. Then, I can do it on my own next time.
W: What does Violet NOT need help with?

W: 엄마와 딸 사이의 대화를 듣고 질문에 답하세요.
G: 엄마, 초콜릿 칩 쿠키 굽는거 도와주실 수 있어요?
W: 물론이지. 무엇을 도와주면 될까?
G: 재료를 계량하는게 너무 어려워요.
W: 그럴 수 있지. 네게 필요한 것은 저울이란다.
G: 고마워요. 저울을 사용하는 법은 알아요! 오븐을 예열하는 것도 도와줄 수 있을까요?
W: 물론이지. 하지만 엄마가 해주는 것 보다 먼저 어떻게 하는지 보여주는게 어떨까?
G: 좋은 생각이예요, 엄마. 그러면 다음에는 제가 스스로 할 수 있을 것 같아요.

W: Violet이 도움을 필요하지 않은 것은 무엇입니까?

(A) 오븐을 데우는 것
(B) 저울을 사용하는 것
(C) 올바르게 계량하는 것

35.
W: Listen to a conversation between a mother and her son. Listen for the answer to this question.
W: Sean, I thought we could go camping at Lake Louis this weekend.
B: Mom, that sounds great! But I thought we were going to go to the Lion King musical.
W: The weather forecast says it will be bright and sunny, so how about we go to the musical next week?
B: Great! Can we build a fire and roast marshmallows?
W: Sure, I know how much you had fun the last time we went.
B: I sure did. It was even more fun because James went with us.
W: Then how about we take James with us again?
B: Thank you, mom! The last time we met, he told me how much he wanted to go with us again.
W: OK, but make sure that you call and ask James first.
W: What will Sean do next?

W: 엄마와 아들 사이의 대화를 듣고 질문에 답하세요.
W: Sean, 우리 이번 주말에 Lake Louis로 캠핑을 가는 거 어때?
B: 좋은 생각이에요! 근데 라이온 킹 뮤지컬에 가기로 했잖아요.
W: 일기예보를 보니 날씨가 맑을 거라고 하더구나. 뮤지컬은 다음주에 보러 가는 게 어떨까?
B: 좋아요! 불을 피워서 마시멜로우를 구워 먹어도 돼요?
W: 그렇게 하자. 저번에 캠핑 갔을 때 네가 얼마나 좋아했는지 알고 있단다.
B: 그럼요. James와 함께 가니 더 재밌었어요.
W: 그러면 이번에도 James와 함께 가는 것은 어떨까?
B: 고마워요, 엄마! 지난번에 만났을 때, James가 우리랑 다시 가고 싶다고 말했어요.
W: 좋아, 먼저 James에게 전화해서 물어보렴.

W: Sean은 다음에 무엇을 할 예정입니까?

(A) James의 집에 가서 그에게 캠핑을 가고 싶은지 물어볼 것이다.
(B) James에게 전화해서 이번 주에 일정이 있냐고 물어볼 것이다.
(C) 그는 마시멜로우를 살 것이다.

Part 5.

36.
W: A guest speaker will come to our school and will be giving a speech. This speaker graduated from our school twenty years ago, and it is her first time visiting as a guest speaker. Please make sure to bring pencils and pens, and something to write on. Also, make sure that you are on time!

W: What should the students bring to the speech?

W: 초청 연설자가 우리 학교에 와서 연설을 할 예정입니다. 이 연사는 20년 전에 우리 학교를 졸업했으며 초청 연사로 방문하는 것은 이번이 처음입니다. 연필과 펜, 그리고 필기할 것을 꼭 챙겨주세요. 또한 제시간에 도착해주세요!

W: 학생들은 연설에 무엇을 가져와야 하나요?

(A) 카메라
(B) 공책
(C) 교과서

37.
G: Mrs. Harrington, hello, it's Shelby calling. Elly left her tennis bag and sweater at my place. I know that she needs them for practice tomorrow. Do you think you can come and pick it up? Or I can give it to her when I see her at practice tomorrow.

W: Why did Shelby call?

G: Harrington 부인, 안녕하세요, Shelby입니다. Elly가 우리 집에 테니스 가방이랑 스웨터를 두고 갔어요. 내일 연습할 때 필요할 것 같아서요. 혹시 가지러 오실 수 있을까요? 아니면 제가 내일 연습할 때 Elly한테 전해줄게요.

W: Shelby는 왜 전화를 했습니까?

(A) Harrington 부인에게 그녀를 데리러 올 수 있는지 물어보기 위해서
(B) Harrington 부인에게 Elly가 그녀의 물건을 두고 왔다는 것을 알려주기 위해
(C) Harrington 부인에게 Elly가 테니스 연습을 해야 한다는 것을 설명하기 위해

38.
G: Hi Julie, it's Olivia. How are you feeling? In class today, we learned about the North and South Poles. Mr. Humphrey told us so much about the poles that we had to take a lot of notes. Since there will be a test on it next week, call me if you need any help.

W: Why did Olivia call?

G: 안녕 Julie, Olivia야. 기분은 어때? 오늘 수업에서 북극과 남극에 대해 배웠어. Humphrey 선생님께서 극지방에 대해 설명을 아주 많이 해주셔서, 필기할게 정말 많았어. 다음 주에 시험이 있으니 도움이 필요하면 전화 해.

W: Olivia는 왜 전화를 했습니까?

(A) Julie에게 오늘 시험을 봤다고 말하기 위해
(B) Julie에게 그녀가 극지방에 대해 발표를 해야 한다고 말하기 위해
(C) 그녀가 수업을 따라잡는 데 도움이 필요한지 확인하기 위해

39.
G: Hi Kate, it's Sara. Did you see all the cherry blossoms outside? It's such a beautiful day. I'm about to go and take the dogs out for a walk. How about we meet at the park and have some ice cream? The ice cream truck has a huge variety. I tried some with my mom last week, and they were super delicious.

W: Why did Sara call?

G: 안녕, Kate, Sara야. 밖에 있는 벚꽃 봤어? 정말 아름다운 날이야. 이제 개들을 데리고 산책하러 가려고 하는데, 공원에서 만나서 아이스크림 먹는 건 어때? 트럭에서 여러 가지 종류의 아이스크림을 팔더라. 지난주에 엄마와 함께 먹어봤는데 정말 맛있었어.

W: Sara는 왜 전화를 했습니까?

(A) Kate에게 개 산책을 시켰다고 말하기 위해
(B) Kate가 아이스크림을 좋아하는지 물어보기 위해
(C) Kate가 공원에 가고 싶어하는지 물어보기 위해

40.
M: Hi David, it's dad. Can you take care of your sister after school today? Your mom and I are running late because of heavy traffic. We'll try to get home as soon as we can.

W: Why did dad call?

M: 안녕 David, 아빠야. 오늘 방과 후에 여동생을 돌봐 줄 수 있어? 엄마와 나는 교통 체증 때문에 늦고 있어. 최대한 빨리 집에 갈 수 있도록 노력해볼게.

W: 아빠는 왜 전화를 했습니까?

(A) David가 여동생을 돌볼 수 있는지 묻기 위해
(B) David가 늦을 것인지 묻기 위해
(C) David가 가능한 집에 빨리 가라고 말하기 위해

41.
W: Hi Matthew. Mom here! I know you're in class and can't pick up. You left your gym bag at home with your baseball uniform. Meet me behind the sports field, and I will drop it off at lunchtime. Don't forget!

W: What did the boy leave behind?

W: 안녕 Matthew. 엄마야! 지금 네가 수업 중이라 전화를 받을 수 없다는 걸 알아. 네 체육 가방이랑 야구 유니폼을 집에 두고 갔더구나. 점심시간에 운동장 뒤에서 만나자. 그때 가방 전해줄게. 잊지마!

W: 소년은 무엇을 두고 왔습니까?

(A) 그의 체육 가방
(B) 그의 야구방망이
(C) 그의 점심

Actual Test 2

Reading

1 (C)	2 (A)	3 (C)	4 (A)
5 (A)	6 (C)	7 (B)	8 (B)
9 (C)	10 (A)	11 (C)	12 (C)
13 (C)	14 (B)	15 (B)	16 (A)
17 (C)	18 (C)	19 (C)	20 (C)
21 (B)	22 (B)	23 (B)	24 (C)
25 (C)	26 (B)	27 (A)	28 (C)
29 (B)	30 (C)	31 (A)	32 (A)
33 (C)	34 (B)	35 (C)	36 (B)
37 (C)	38 (C)	39 (C)	

Part 1.

1. (A) 가족이 점심을 먹고 있다.
   (B) 가족이 저녁을 만들고 있다.
   (C) 가족이 저녁을 먹고 있다.

2. (A) 좁은
   (B) 넓은
   (C) 폭이 넓은

3. (A) 지렁이
   (B) 개미
   (C) 무당벌레

4. (A) 정사각형
   (B) 삼각형
   (C) 직사각형

5. (A) 밀다
   (B) 당기다
   (C) 끌다

6. (A) 도마뱀
   (B) 애벌레
   (C) 악어

7. (A) 더러운
   (B) 깨끗한
   (C) 어두운

8. (A) (표면에 접촉하지 않고) 위에
   (B) 아래에
   (C) (표면에 접촉하고) 위에

9. (A) 더 작은
   (B) 똑같은
   (C) 더 큰

10. (A) 옆에
    (B) 위에
    (C) 안에

11. (A) 운전사
    (B) 탐정(형사)
    (C) 치과의사

12. (A) 잡다
    (B) 던지다
    (C) 차다

13. (A) 고양이는 소파 옆에 앉아있다.
    (B) 개는 소파 위에 앉아있다.
    (C) 개는 소파 옆에 앉아있다.

14. (A) Lina의 아빠는 그의 신발끈을 묶고 있다.
    (B) Lina의 아빠는 Lina의 신발끈을 묶어주고 있다.
    (C) Lina는 그녀의 신발끈을 묶으려고 하고 있다.

15. (A) City Bank는 호텔 옆에 있다.
    (B) 호텔은 도서관 맞은 편에 있다.
    (C) 도서관은 주유소 뒤에 있다.

16. (A) 새들이 나뭇가지 위에 앉아있다.
    (B) 새들이 하늘을 날고 있는 중이다.
    (C) 새들이 둥지를 만들고 있는 중이다.

17. (A) 소녀는 과일과 채소를 파는 중이다.
    (B) 남자는 과일과 채소를 요리하는 중이다.
    (C) 소녀는 과일과 채소를 사는 중이다.

Part 2.

18. 그는 우유를 마시려고 합니다. 그는 우유를 붓기 위해 이것이 필요합니다. 이것은 주로 부엌에 있습니다. 이것은 무엇일까요?

    (A) 접시
    (B) 숟가락
    (C) 컵

19. 이것은 다른 종류의 식물과 채소를 먹습니다. 이것은 작고 털이 많고 긴 귀를 가지고 있습니다. 이것은 빨리 달릴 수 있고 깡총 뛰어다닙니다. 이것은 무엇일까요?

    (A) 생쥐
    (B) 여우
    (C) 토끼

20. 사람들은 이것으로 장거리를 여행합니다. 그것들은 길고 많은 좌석을 가지고 있습니다. 그것은 트랙 위를 달리며 많은 사람들을 운송합니다. 그것은 무엇일까요?

    (A) 비행기
    (B) 버스
    (C) 기차

21. 그는 직사각형 물체를 그의 귀에 대고 있습니다. 그는 누군가에게 얘기를 하는 중이고, 행복해 보입니다. 그는 _____.

    (A) 책을 읽고 있는 중이다.
    (B) 통화를 하는 중이다.
    (C) 영화를 보는 중이다.

22. 그녀는 붓을 사용하고 있습니다. 그녀는 붓을 다른 물감에 담그고 있습니다. 그림에는 귀여운 개가 그려져 있습니다. 그녀는 _____.

    (A) 쓰는 중이다.
    (B) 그리는 중이다.
    (C) 자르는 중이다.

23. 사람들은 이것을 태양(해)로부터 그들의 피부를 지키기 위해 필요합니다. 이것은 로션이나 스프레이 같이 다른 종류로 있습니다. 이것은 무엇일까요?

    (A) 선글라스
    (B) 자외선 차단제
    (C) 햇빛

24. 당신은 단어의 의미를 모릅니다. 선생님께 물어보려 하지만 선생님은 바쁘십니다. 당신은 사전을 찾습니다.
    당신은 단어의 의미를 _____.

    (A) 골라낸다
    (B) 과시하다
    (C) 찾아보다

25. 소녀는 수학 문제를 풀려고 노력하는 중입니다. 비록 그녀가 힘든 시간을 보내고 있지만, 계속해서 시도하고 있는 중입니다. 그 소녀는 _____이 아닙니다.

    (A) 골라내는 중
    (B) 거절하는 중
    (C) 포기하는 중

26. 사람들은 음식을 차갑고 신선하게 보관하기 위해 이것에 넣습니다. 또한 음식이 상하는 것을 방지하는 데 도움이 됩니다. 아이스크림과 같은 것을 얼리는 공간도 있습니다. 그것은 무엇일까요?

    (A) 오븐
    (B) 냉장고
    (C) 식기세척기

27. 당신은 길을 걷고 있습니다. 당신은 아는 사람을 알아봅니다. 이 사람에게 손을 흔들기 시작합니다.

당신은 아는 누군가를 _____.

(A) 마주치다
(B) 변하다
(C) 찾아보다

Part 3.

[28-31] 아래를 읽고, 28-31번 질문에 답하세요.

벨라의 방과 후 일정표						
날짜	월	화	수	목	금
오후 3시	과학 동아리	테니스 동아리 - 경기를 위해 연습하기	연극 동아리 - 학교에서	숙제하기	놀기
오후 5시	청소하기 - 엄마가 설거지 하는 것 도와드리기	저녁 먹기	놀기	독서 동아리 - 도서관에서	놀기
오후 7시	저녁 먹기	숙제 하기	저녁 먹기	댄스 동아리	저녁 먹기 - 조부모님과 저녁 먹기
오후 8시	가족 시간 갖기 - 스크래블 & 보드게임	잠자기	씻기	저녁 먹기	가족 시간 갖기

28. Bella는 수요일에 어떤 동아리에 갑니까?

(A) 테니스 동아리
(B) 독서 동아리
(C) 연극 동아리

29. Bella는 금요일에 저녁을 몇 시에 먹습니까?

(A) 오후 5시
(B) 오후 7시
(C) 오후 8시

30. Bella에게는 언제 두 번의 놀이 시간이 있습니까?

(A) 월요일마다
(B) 수요일마다
(C) 금요일마다

31. Bella는 화요일에 오후 7시에 무엇을 합니까?

(A) 숙제 하기

(B) 저녁 먹기
(C) 자러 가기

[32-35] 다음 초대장을 보고, 32-35번 질문에 답하세요.

South Westwick 졸업 파티

South Westwick 교사들은 특별한 추억을 만들면서 즐겁고 신나는 시간을 가지기 위하여 모든 졸업생들을 초대합니다.

우리 모두는 열심히 노력한 훌륭한 여러분을 자랑스럽게 생각합니다. 여러분의 우정과 함께한 멋진 추억을 축하하고 싶습니다.
초등학교 시절의 마지막을 축하하러 오세요!

졸업 파티 스케줄

페이스 페인팅	도서관 : 1층	오후 2:00 – 3:30
사진 부스	체육관 : 2층	하루 종일
시상식	강당 : 3층	오후 4:00 – 5:00
풍선 터트리기	체육관 : 2층	오후 5:00 – 5:30
댄스 파티	강당 : 3층	오후 5:30 – 7:00

모든 가족 구성원이 이 파티에 초대되었으니, 이 특별한 행사에 참석하여 축하해 주시기 바랍니다.

체육관에 파티음식이 준비되어 있고, 음료와 맛있는 케이크가 포함되어 있습니다.

---

32. 시간 일정이 없는 활동은 무엇입니까?

(A) 사진 부스
(B) 상장 시상식
(C) 댄스 파티

33. 상장은 어디에서 수여되나요?

(A) 체육관에서
(B) 주차장에서
(C) 강당에서

34. 음료는 어디에서 받을 수 있나요?

(A) 1층
(B) 2층
(C) 3층

35. 학교가 졸업 파티를 개최하려는 이유는 무엇입니까?

(A) 학생들이 고등학교로 가는 것을 축하하기 위해
(B) 학생들이 대회에서 이긴 것을 축하하기 위해
(C) 학생들의 노력에 대해 칭찬하기 위해

[36-37] 이메일을 읽고, 36-37번 질문에 답하세요.

> 받는 사람: Lina
> 보내는 사람: Jordan
> 주제: 이번 주말 계획
>
> Lina에게,
> 지난주 피아노 콘서트에서 뛰어난 공연 축하해. 너의 재능은 정말 인상적이고 앞으로의 공연에서도 계속 성공하길 빌어!
> 휴식을 위해 이번 주말에 나와 크리스와 함께 아이스 스케이팅을 하러 갈래? 새로운 아이스링크가 정말 크고 눈 축제도 열린다고 들었어. 눈사람도 만들고 아이스하키도 할 수 있어.
> 우리는 오전 10시에 출발해서 오후 7시쯤 돌아올 계획이야. 올 수 있다면, 오전 9시 30분에 학교 앞에서 만나. 올 수 있는지 알려줘!
>
> Jordan으로부터

36. 왜 Jordan은 Lina에게 편지를 썼습니까?

   (A) 그녀의 스케이트를 빌릴 수 있는지 물어보기 위해
   (B) 그녀가 이번 주에 아이스 스케이팅을 타러 갈 수 있는지 물어보기 위해
   (C) 그녀가 아이스 하키를 할 수 있는지 물어보기 위해서

37. 그들은 언제 집으로 돌아올 예정입니까?

   (A) 대략 오전 10시
   (B) 오전 9시 반쯤
   (C) 대략 오후 7시

[38-39] 편지를 읽고, 38-39번 질문에 답하세요.

> Williams부인께,
> 안녕하세요, Daisy입니다. 동물 동면에 대한 연설이 얼마나 도움이 되었는지 몰라요. 동물들이 깊은 잠에 들기 전 지방을 저장하기 위해 엄청난 양의 음식을 먹는다는 사실이 매우 흥미로웠어요. 또한 체온이 떨어지고 호흡 속도가 느려진다는 사실도요!
> 더 많은 연설에 등록하고 싶어요! 사실 다음 달에 공룡에 대한 연설이 있다는 소식을 아빠에게서 들었어요. 참석하기 전에 공룡에 대해 자세히 공부하도록 할게요. 다시 한 번 환상적인 연설에 감사드립니다!
>
> 진심을 담아, Daisy올림.

38. 동물들이 동면 중에 일어나지 않는 것은 무엇입니까?

   (A) 체온이 떨어진다.
   (B) 호흡의 속도가 느려진다.
   (C) 엄청난 양의 음식을 먹는다.

39. Daisy는 다음 연설을 신청하기 전에 무엇을 할 예정입니까?

   (A) 동면에 관한 연설문을 쓸 것이다.
   (B) 동면에 접어드는 동물들에 관한 비디오를 볼 것이다.
   (C) 고대 생물에 대해 공부한다.

Listening

1	(B)	2	(B)	3	(A)	4	(C)
5	(C)	6	(C)	7	(B)	8	(C)
9	(C)	10	(C)	11	(C)	12	(C)
13	(B)	14	(C)	15	(C)	16	(B)
17	(A)	18	(B)	19	(C)	20	(B)
21	(C)	22	(A)	23	(C)	24	(B)
25	(A)	26	(C)	27	(C)	28	(C)
29	(B)	30	(A)	31	(A)	32	(C)
33	(C)	34	(B)	35	(B)	36	(C)
37	(C)	38	(A)	39	(C)	40	(C)
41	(C)						

Part 1.

1. She is picking up her jacket.

   그녀는 그녀의 자켓을 집어 드는 중이다.

2. He is putting on his helmet.

   그는 그의 헬멧을 쓰고 있는 중이다.

3. The pink vase is bigger than the white vase.

   분홍색 꽃병은 하얀색 꽃병보다 더 크다.

4. The park is between many buildings.

   공원은 많은 건물들 사이에 있다.

5. She is walking a dog.

   그녀는 개를 산책 시키고 있는 중이다.

6. The girl is sending a letter.

   소녀는 편지를 보내고 있는 중이다.

7. He is choosing new furniture.

   그는 새로운 가구를 고르는 중이다.

8. The car is NOT clean.

   차가 깨끗하지 않다.

Part 2.

9.
W: Listen to a teacher.
M: Make sure that you are all ready to go to the zoo. The school bus will be here any minute.
W: What did the teacher tell his students to do?

W: 선생님이 하는 얘기를 들어보세요.
M: 동물원에 갈 준비가 모두 되었는지 확인하세요. 곧 스쿨버스가 도착할 것입니다.
W: 선생님은 학생들에게 무엇을 하라고 했습니까?

10.
W: Listen to a teacher in geography class.
W: Today, we will learn how to read maps and use a compass. Please take out your compass from your bags.
W: What did the teacher ask her students to do?

W: 지리 시간에 선생님이 하는 얘기를 들어보세요.
W: 오늘은 지도를 읽고 나침반을 사용하는 방법을 배워보겠습니다. 가방에서 나침반을 꺼내 보세요.
W: 선생님은 학생들에게 무엇을 하라고 했습니까?

11.
W: Listen to a boy.
B: Mom, can you take me to school today? I missed the school bus and it's raining hard outside.
W: What did the son ask his mother to do?

W: 소년이 하는 얘기를 들어보세요.
B: 엄마, 오늘 학교에 데려다 줄 수 있어요? 스쿨버스를 놓쳤는데 밖에 비가 너무 많이 와요.
W: 소년은 엄마에게 무엇을 부탁하였습니까?

12.
W: Listen to a father.
M: Oliver, well done in finishing your writing for your speech! Now, we're going to practice memorizing your writing. Make sure that you speak loudly and clearly.
W: What did the father tell his son to do?

W: 아빠가 하는 얘기를 들어보세요.
M: Oliver, 연설을 위한 글을 마무리하느라 수고했어! 이제 글을 외우는 연습을 해볼거야. 반드시 크고 명확하게 말하렴.
W: 아빠는 아들에게 무엇을 하라고 했습니까?

13.
W: Listen to a girl.
G: Mom and I went shopping. Although I wanted to swim with dad, he got home from work too late, so we couldn't go.
W: What did the girl do with her mom?

W: 소녀가 하는 얘기를 들어보세요.
G: 엄마와 저는 쇼핑을 하러 갔어요. 비록 제가 아빠와 수영하기를 원했지만, 아빠는 일 때문에 집에 늦게 오셔서 우리는 갈 수 없었어요.
W: 소녀는 엄마와 무엇을 했습니까?

14.
W: Listen to a boy.
B: Bella, you are such a great swimmer. I can't swim without a swim ring. Can you show me how to use both my arms and legs in the water?
W: What did the boy ask the girl to do?

W: 소년이 하는 얘기를 들어보세요.
B: Bella, 너는 수영을 정말 잘하는구나. 나는 튜브 없이는 수영을 할 수 없어. 물 속에서 팔과 다리를 사용하는 방법을 알려 줄 수 있니?
W: 소년은 소녀에게 무엇을 요청했습니까?

15.
W: Listen to a boy.
B: Mom, can we go and take Emma out for a walk? We couldn't take her out yesterday because it was raining. I think she really wants to play fetch.
W: What did the boy ask his mother to do?

W: 소년이 하는 얘기를 들어보세요.
B: 엄마, Emma를 데리고 산책하러 가도 될까요? 어제 비가 와서 Emma를 데리고 나갈 수 없었어요. Emma는 정말 fetch 놀이를 하고 싶어하는 것 같아요.
W: 소년은 엄마에게 무엇을 부탁하였습니까?

16.
W: Listen to a teacher in math class.
W: We're going to learn multiplication today. We're not going to use our calculators, so please put them away.
W: What did the teacher ask the students to do?

W: 수학 시간에 선생님이 하는 얘기를 들어보세요.
W: 오늘은 곱셈을 배울 거예요. 계산기는 사용하지 않으니 치워주세요.
W: 선생님은 학생들에게 무엇을 하라고 했습니까?

17.
W: Listen to a mother.
W: Violet, can you call your dad and ask if he can pick up your sister on his way home? I just got a call from your sister's teacher saying that Kylie is not feeling well.
W: What did the mother tell her daughter to do?

W: 엄마가 하는 얘기를 들어보세요.
W: Violet, 아빠에게 전화해서 오는 길에 동생을 데리고 오실 수 있는지 물어봐줄래? 방금 동생의 선생님께서 Kylie의 몸이 안 좋다는 연락을 받았거든.
W: 엄마는 딸에게 무엇을 하라고 부탁하였습니까?

18.
W: Listen to a mother.
W: Kate, you've done a great job. Now that you have finished shaping the clay, we have to wait a couple of days for it to dry completely before putting it in the oven to harden.
W: What did the mother tell her daughter to do?

W: 엄마가 하는 얘기를 들어보세요.
W: Kate, 정말 수고 많았어. 이제 점토로 모양을 잡는 것을 마쳤으니, 오븐에 넣고 단단해지기 전에 완전히 마를 때까지 이틀을 기다려야 한단다.
W: 엄마는 딸에게 무엇을 하라고 했습니까?

19.
W: Listen to a science teacher.
M: We have a very special class planned for the day. We will wear gloves and boots to go outside and plant a tree. Trees are called the lungs of the Earth because they absorb CO_2 from the atmosphere and supply oxygen for people.
W: What did the teacher tell his students to do?

W: 과학 선생님이 하는 얘기를 들어보세요.
M: 오늘은 매우 특별한 수업을 계획하고 있어요. 장갑과 장화를 신고 밖으로 나가 나무를 심을 예정입니다. 나무는 대기에서 이산화탄소를 흡수하고 사람들에게 산소를 공급하기 때문에 지구의 허파라고 불린답니다.
W: 선생님은 학생들에게 무엇을 하라고 했습니까?

Part 3.

20.
G: What did you have for breakfast?
(A) With my grandparents.
(B) I didn't have any.
(C) In an hour.

G: 너는 아침으로 무엇을 먹었니?
(A) 조부모님과 함께 먹었어.
(B) 나는 먹지 않았어.
(C) 한 시간 내로 먹을 거야.

[21-23] Listen to a boy talking to his friend.
소년이 친구에게 하는 얘기를 들어보세요.

21.
B: Thank you for explaining how to solve this math problem.
(A) No problem. Dictionaries are a great help.
(B) You're welcome. Watching the news is important.
(C) Anytime. Ask me whenever you need help.

B: 나에게 이 수학 문제를 풀 수 있도록 설명해줘서 고마워.
(A) 천만에. 사전은 큰 도움이 돼.
(B) 천만에. 뉴스를 보는 것은 중요해.
(C) 언제든지 도움이 필요하면 물어봐.

22.
B: Actually, can you help me mark my vocabulary test?
(A) Absolutely, let's take a look.
(B) That sounds great, I need your help.
(C) That's right, studying vocabulary is very important.

B: 저기, 단어 시험지 채점하는 것을 도와줄 수 있니?
(A) 물론이지. 한 번 보자.
(B) 좋아. 나는 너의 도움이 필요해.
(C) 맞아. 단어 공부를 하는 것은 매우 중요해.

23.
B: Can you lend me your red pen?
(A) You can lend me one.
(B) No, I can.
(C) Sorry, I only have a black one.

B: 나에게 너의 빨간펜을 빌려줄 수 있니?
(A) 나한테 하나 빌려줄 수 있어.
(B) 아니, 빌려줄게.
(C) 미안, 나는 검은색 펜 밖에 없어.

[24-26] Listen to a dad talking to his son.
아빠가 아들에게 하는 얘기를 들어보세요.

24.
M: Do you have everything for tennis practice?
(A) Please sit down, everyone.
(B) I think I packed everything.
(C) I'm sure you're ready to perform.

M: 테니스 연습 가기 위해 다 챙겼니?
(A) 모두들 앉아주세요.
(B) 제가 생각하기에 다 챙긴 것 같아요.
(C) 저는 아빠가 칠 준비가 되어 있다고 확신해요.

25.
M: Which bag is yours?
(A) It's the one on the right.
(B) I can't fit anything more in.
(C) Thank you, you found it.

M: 어떤 가방이 너의 것이니?
(A) 오른쪽에 있는 거예요.
(B) 더 이상 안 들어가요.
(C) 고마워요. 아빠가 찾아 주었네요.

26.

M: Should I wait for you in the car?

(A) It takes about thirty minutes.
(B) It's not that big anyway.
(C) No, I won't be long.

M: 내가 차 안에서 너를 기다릴까?

(A) 30분 정도 걸려요.
(B) 어차피 안 커요.
(C) 아니요, 오래 걸리지 않을 거예요.

Part 4.

27.

W: Listen to a conversation between a boy and girl. Listen for the answer to this question.

B: Are you looking for something?
G: I'm trying to find my glasses.
B: I think you left them at the gym.
G: That's right! I took them off before playing dodgeball.
W: Where will the girl go next?

W: 소년과 소녀 사이의 대화를 듣고 질문에 답하세요.

B: 뭐 찾고 있어?
G: 안경을 찾고 있어.
B: 체육관에 두고 온 거 아니야?
G: 맞아! 피구를 하기 전에 벗었어.

W: 소녀는 다음에 어디로 갈까요?

(A) 가서 피구를 할 것이다.
(B) 소년을 도와 그가 안경을 찾는 것을 도와줄 것이다.
(C) 체육관에 갈 것이다.

28.

W: Listen to a conversation between a mother and her daughter. Listen for the answer to this question.

G: Can I take violin lessons, Mom? My friend Bonnie told me how fun it is.
W: But you've only just started learning to play the piano.
G: I know, but playing the piano is so difficult. I still have trouble reading the notes.
W: Then, how about you try your best for three more months and then we can talk about it again.
G: OK, that's a promise.
W: What will the girl do next?

W: 엄마와 딸 사이의 대화를 듣고 질문에 답하세요.

G: 엄마, 바이올린 레슨을 받을 수 있을까요? 제 친구 Bonnie가 바이올린 레슨이 얼마나 재미있는지 말해줬어요.
W: 하지만 이제 막 피아노를 배우기 시작했잖니.
G: 알아요, 하지만 피아노 연주는 정말 어려워요. 아직 음표를 읽는 데 어려움을 겪고 있어요.
W: 그럼 3개월 더 최선을 다하고 나서 다시 이야기하는 건 어떨까.
G: 네, 약속해요.

W: 소녀는 다음에 무엇을 하나요?

(A) 바이올린을 최선을 다해서 연주한다.
(B) 3달 동안 바이올린 레슨을 받는다.
(C) 피아노를 배우는 데 노력을 한다.

29.

W: Listen to a conversation between a mother and her daughter. Listen for the answer to this question.

W: What are you up to, Ellie?
G: Grandma's birthday is coming up, so I decided to do something special for her.
W: What a thoughtful idea. Is that the birthday card? Those paper flowers look lovely.
G: Yes, you know how much grandma loves roses.
W: It looks great! Do you need help gluing them?
G: No thank you, I think I can do it, but I need to cut them first.
W: I'm proud of how you're trying to finish it all by yourself.
G: Thanks, mom, but actually, can you go and pick up grandma's cake from the bakery?
W: Oh, my goodness, I completely forgot about that. I'll go right away.
W: What will the woman do next?

W: 엄마와 딸 사이의 대화를 듣고 질문에 답하세요.

W: Ellie, 지금 뭐하는 중이야?
G: 할머니 생신이 다가와서 할머니를 위해 특별한 일을 해드리기로 했어요.
W: 정말 사려 깊구나. 그게 생일 카드이니? 종이 꽃이 정말 멋져 보이네.
G: 네, 할머니께서 장미를 얼마나 좋아하시는지 아시죠.
W: 멋져 보이네! 붙이는 데 도움이 필요하니?
G: 아니요, 괜찮아요. 할 수 있을 것 같은데 먼저 잘라야 해요.
W: 혼자서 모든 것을 끝내려고 노력하는 모습이 자랑스럽구나.
G: 엄마, 고마워요. 그런데 빵집에서 할머니 케이크를 찾아주실 수 있어요?
W: 세상에, 그걸 완전히 잊어버렸구나. 바로 다녀오마.

W: 엄마는 다음에 무엇을 할 것입니까?

(A) 종이꽃을 붙일 것이다.
(B) 빵집에 들러 케이크를 가져올 것이다.
(C) Ellie가 그녀의 선물을 마무리하는 것을 도울 것이다.

30.

W: Listen to a conversation between a mother and her son. Listen for the answer to this question.
B: I don't want to wear a jacket today. It's not that cold.
W: I heard that it's going to rain in the afternoon.
B: Yeah, but the weather forecast is not always right.
W: I know, but I want you to take it with you anyway. I don't want you getting a cold.
B: OK, I'll wear it. I sure don't want to catch a cold. But mom, I don't know where my jacket is.
W: It's over there in the closet, next to your blue sweater.
B: Thank you mom. I'll go and get it.
W: What will the boy do next?

W: 엄마와 아들 사이의 대화를 듣고 질문에 답하세요.

B: 오늘은 재킷을 입고 싶지 않아요. 그렇게 춥지 않거든요.
W: 오후에 비가 온다는구나.
B: 네, 하지만 일기 예보가 항상 맞는 것은 아니에요.
W: 알아, 하지만 어쨌든 감기에 걸리지 않도록 가지고 가는 것이 좋을 것 같다.
B: 알겠어요, 입을게요. 감기에 걸리고 싶지 않아요. 하지만 엄마, 제 재킷이 어디 있는지 모르겠어요.
W: 저기 옷장 안, 파란색 스웨터 옆에 있단다.
B: 고마워요, 엄마. 제가 가서 가져올 게요.

W: 소년은 다음에 무엇을 할 것입니까?

(A) 그의 자켓을 찾을 것이다.
(B) 엄마에게 그의 파란색 스웨터를 찾아달라고 요청할 것이다.
(C) 밖으로 나갈 것이다.

31.

W: Listen to a conversation between a father and his daughter. Listen for the answer to this question.
M: Ellie, can you help your mom do the dishes?
G: She's already done! I even helped her dry them.
M: I'm proud, Ellie! As a treat, how about we go to the movies?
G: I want to but I have to finish my science project first.
M: How long do you think it will take?
G: Hmm, an hour? Maybe two?
M: Then how about we go afterwards? I'll be in the garage fixing your bike.
G: That sounds wonderful, dad.
W: What does the girl have to do first?

W: 아빠와 딸 사이의 대화를 듣고 질문에 답하세요.

M: Ellie, 엄마가 설거지하는 것 좀 도와줄 수 있니?
G: 엄마가 이미 다 했어요! 제가 그릇들을 닦는 것도 도와드렸어요.
M: 자랑스럽구나, Ellie. 보상으로 영화 보러 가는 건 어떠니?
G: 그러고 싶지만 먼저 과학 프로젝트를 끝내야 해요.
M: 얼마나 걸릴 것 같니?
G: 음, 한 시간? 아니면 두 시간?
M: 그럼 끝나고 가는 건 어때? 차고에서 자전거를 수리하고 있으마.
G: 아빠, 정말 좋은 생각이에요.

W: 소녀가 먼저 해야 할 일은 무엇입니까?

(A) 그녀의 과학 프로젝트를 끝낼 것이다.
(B) 설거지하는 것을 끝낼 것이다.
(C) 영화 보러 갈 준비를 할 것이다.

32.

W: Listen to a conversation between two students. Listen for the answer to this question.
B: How was your trip to California?
G: It was so much fun! I saw the Golden Gate Bridge, and even learned how to surf.
B: I love surfing! Was it your first time?
G: You bet it was. I loved it so much that I want to try again.
B: I know the feeling, but wasn't it hard to keep your balance?
G: It was at first, but I met a great teacher, and she showed me the basics in a fun way.
B: You're so lucky! I always have trouble standing up. How about we go together next time?
G: Absolutely, I'll go and ask mom right away.
W: What did the girl have trouble doing at first?

W: 두 학생 사이의 대화를 듣고, 질문에 답하세요.

B: 캘리포니아 여행은 어땠어?
G: 정말 재미있었어! 금문교도 보고 서핑도 배웠어.
B: 나는 서핑을 정말 좋아해! 처음 해본 거니?
G: 맞아. 정말 마음에 들어서 다시 해보고 싶어.
B: 나도 무슨 말 인지 알지. 그런데 균형을 잡는 것이 어렵지 않았어?
G: 처음에는 그랬지만, 훌륭한 선생님을 만났는데 재미있게 기본기를 보여주셨어.
B: 정말 운이 좋네! 나는 항상 일어서기가 힘들어. 다음에 같이 가는 건 어때?
G: 물론이지, 바로 가서 엄마에게 여쭤볼게.

W: 소녀는 처음에 무엇을 하는데 어려움을 겪었습니까?

(A) 소년에게 서핑하는 방법을 가르쳐 주는 것
(B) 좋은 선생님을 만난 것
(C) 서핑 보드 위에서 서있는 것

33.

W: Listen to a conversation between two students. Listen for the answer to this question.

G: Wow! That statue made from recycled materials looks amazing.

B: I know, I can't believe that it was made from reused goods.

G: I wonder who made it.

B: I don't know but whoever did, has great talent. I think this statue will help people to understand how goods that have already been used can be turned into something great.

G: I agree, it has made me think outside the box. In fact, when I get home, I want to make something out of recycled goods.

B: Do you have anything in mind?

G: It's a secret! I'll show you when I'm done.

B: Great, show it to me once you're finished.

W: What does the girl want to do?

W: 두 학생 사이의 대화를 듣고, 질문에 답하세요.

G: 왜! 재활용 재료로 만든 저 동상 정말 멋져 보인다.

B: 내말이, 재사용된 물건으로 만들었다는 게 믿기지 않아.

G: 누가 만들었는지 궁금하네.

B: 잘 모르겠지만 누가 그랬던 훌륭한 재능을 가지고 있는 것 같아. 이 동상은 이미 사용된 상품이 어떻게 훌륭한 것으로 변할 수 있는지 사람들이 이해하는 데 도움이 될 것이라고 생각해.

G: 나도 동의해. 그래서 틀에서 벗어난 생각을 하게 되었어. 집에 돌아가면 재활용품으로 무언가를 만들고 싶어.

B: 마음에 두고 있는 것이 있어?

G: 비밀이야! 끝나면 보여줄게.

B: 좋아, 끝나면 보여줘.

W: 소녀는 무엇을 하고 싶어 하나요?

(A) 재활용품으로 만들어진 동상을 사고 싶어한다.
(B) 집에 가서 그녀가 만든 것을 소년에게 보여주고 싶어한다.
(C) 재생용품으로 무언가를 만들고 싶어 한다.

Part 5.

34.

M: Hello, it's Mr. Simpson. A quick reminder to tell you that we have a fire drill practice today. There will be no recess, so make sure to have lunch before then, and be back in your classrooms by one o'clock. The practice will take around half an hour.

W: What should students do first?

M: 안녕하세요, Simpson입니다. 오늘 소방 훈련 연습이 있다는 사실을 알려드립니다. 쉬는 시간이 없으니 그 전에 점심을 먹고 1시까지 교실로 돌아오세요. 연습은 약 30분 정도 소요될 예정입니다.

W: 학생들이 먼저 해야 할 것은 무엇입니까?

(A) 소방 훈련에 참여하기
(B) 점심을 먹기
(C) 휴식을 취하기

35.

G: Hi Aileen, it's Agnes calling. I know we were meeting up at your place first, but can we meet up at the mall instead? I need to buy school supplies.

W: Why did Agnes call?

G: 안녕, Aileen. 나 Agnes야. 먼저 너의 집에서 만나기로 한 걸로 알고 있는데, 대신 쇼핑몰에서 만날 수 있을까? 학교에서 쓸 학용품을 사야 해.

W: Agnes는 왜 전화를 했습니까?

(A) Aileen이 학용품을 가져오도록 요청하려고
(B) 쇼핑몰에서 만날 수 있는지 물어보기 위해서
(C) Aileen에게 자기가 그녀의 집에 있을 거라고 말해주기 위해

36.

B: Hey Leo, it's James. I heard that there is going to be a Bug Science Fair in two weeks. I know we have to do a project about insects at school, so I was wondering if you want to go with me. The tickets are first come, first served, so please get back to me right away!

W: Why does Leo have to call James as soon as possible?

B: 안녕 Leo, 나야 James. 2주 후에 곤충 과학 박람회가 열린다고 들었어. 학교에서 곤충에 관한 프로젝트를 해야 한다고 알고 있는데, 같이 가고 싶은지 궁금해. 티켓은 선착순이니 빨리 연락해 줘!

W: Leo가 왜 가능한 한 빨리 James에게 전화해야 하나요?

(A) 그가 얼마나 곤충을 좋아하는지 말해주기 위해
(B) 그가 곤충 과학 박람회를 가기를 원하는지 물어보기 위해
(C) 티켓이 완판 되기 전에 예약을 하기 위해

37.

G: Dad, it's Lucy. I'm at Sally's place, but things are taking longer than expected. I'm sorry, but could you pick me up an hour later? We still haven't finished our group project, and it's taking longer than planned.

W: Why did Lucy call dad?

G: 아빠, Lucy예요. Sally 집에 왔는데 예상보다 오래 걸리고 있어요. 죄송하지만, 1시간 후에 데리러 오실 수 있어요? 아직 그룹 프로젝트가 끝나지 않았고, 계획보다 시간이 오래 걸리고 있어요.

W: Lucy는 왜 아빠에게 전화했습니까?

(A) Sally의 집에서 하룻밤을 보내야 했다.
(B) Sally와 그룹 프로젝트를 하기로 결정했다.
(C) 나중에 아빠에게 픽업을 요청했다.

38.

G: Hi Olivia, it's Sophia calling. I just wanted to tell you that you did a fantastic job at the musical yesterday. Your performance was amazing, and you sang the songs perfectly. In fact, you held everyone's attention. I can't wait to see your next performance in two months!

W: Why did Sophia call?

G: 안녕 Olivia. 나 Sophia야. 어제 뮤지컬에서 환상적인 공연을 했다고 말해주고 싶었어. 공연도 훌륭했고 노래도 완벽하게 불렀어. 너는 모두의 관심을 끌었어. 두 달 후의 다음 공연이 정말 기대돼!

W: Sophia는 왜 전화를 했습니까?

(A) Olivia의 공연을 칭찬하기 위해
(B) Olivia를 공연에 초대하기 위해
(C) Olivia에게 다음 공연에 초대해 달라고 요청하기 위해

39.

W: Mrs. Courtney, this is Principal Abrahams. Thank you again for volunteering at the school charity fund last week. It wouldn't have been such a great success if it weren't for your help. The money raised will go to the Education for All charity today. I heard that you would like to visit there with us. The teachers will all be meeting at the center. How about we go together? I'll be waiting for you at the school parking lot.

W: Where will the teachers be meeting?

W: Courtney 부인, Abrahams 교장입니다. 지난주 학교 자선 기금에 자원해 주셔서 다시 한 번 감사드립니다. 부인의 도움이 없었다면 이렇게 큰 성공을 거둘 수 없었을 것입니다. 모금된 기금은 오늘 '모두를 위한 교육' 자선단체에 기부될 예정입니다. 저는 부인께서 저희와 함께 방문하고 싶다고 들었습니다. 선생님들은 모두 센터에서 모일 예정입니다. 같이 가는 건 어떨까요? 학교 주차장에서 기다리고 있겠습니다.

W: 선생님들은 어디에서 만날 예정입니까?

(A) 학교 주차장에서
(B) 자선 단체에서
(C) 자선 단체 센터에서

40.

W: Mrs. Jones, this is Mrs. Moore calling to congratulate Aaron. He won the Spelling Bee contest at school. In fact, he was the only boy who made it to the finals! He did an excellent job of remembering all the words I handed out in class. Please tell Aaron that he will be receiving a trophy in assembly on Monday.

W: Why did Mrs. Moore call Mrs. Jones?

W: Jones 부인, Aaron을 축하하기 위해 전화한 Moore입니다. 그는 학교에서 열린 철자 맞추기 대회에서 우승했습니다. 사실 그는 결승에 진출한 유일한 소년이었어요! 제가 수업 중에 나눠준 모든 단어를 잘 기억해냈어요. Aaron에게 월요일 조회 시간에 트로피를 받게 될 거라고 전해주세요.

W: Moore 부인은 왜 Jones 부인에게 전화를 했습니까?

(A) 월요일에 그녀를 조회시간에 초대하기 위해
(B) 스펠링 대회에서 우승한 그녀를 축하하기 위해
(C) 대회에서 우승한 Aaron을 칭찬하기 위해

41.

M: Listen, everyone! We all must stay together. If you dawdle, we will have to spend time looking for you, which means you'll be late getting back to school. OK, let's start.

W: Why did the guide make the announcement?

M: 여러분! 우리는 모두 함께 다녀야 합니다. 꾸물거리면, 여러분을 찾느라 시간을 보내야 하고, 그러면 학교에 늦게 도착하게 될 거예요. 좋아, 시작합시다.

W: 가이드가 안내방송을 한 이유는 무엇입니까?

(A) 어디로 가야 할 지 설명하기 위해
(B) 그 반 학생들에게 떠나라고 말하기 위해
(C) 단체로 같이 다녀야 한다고 말하기 위해

Actual Test 3

Reading

1	(A)	2	(A)	3	(A)	4	(C)
5	(B)	6	(A)	7	(C)	8	(B)
9	(B)	10	(C)	11	(B)	12	(A)
13	(B)	14	(A)	15	(B)	16	(C)
17	(A)	18	(C)	19	(C)	20	(A)
21	(C)	22	(A)	23	(B)	24	(C)
25	(A)	26	(A)	27	(C)	28	(B)
29	(B)	30	(A)	31	(C)	32	(A)
33	(C)	34	(B)	35	(B)	36	(A)
37	(B)	38	(C)	39	(A)		

Part 1.

1. (A) 그녀는 피곤하다.
   (B) 그녀는 슬프다.
   (C) 그녀는 신이 난다.

2. (A) 동쪽
   (B) 서쪽
   (C) 남쪽

3. (A) 헬멧
   (B) 하프
   (C) 고리

4. (A) 두더지
   (B) 원숭이
   (C) 쥐

5. (A) 파도
   (B) 바람
   (C) 소원

6. (A) 그림자
   (B) 모래
   (C) 이야기

7. (A) 용
   (B) 사슴
   (C) 잠자리

8. (A) 두꺼운
   (B) 얇은
   (C) 무거운

9. (A) 가지고 가다
   (B) 넣다
   (C) 덮다

10. (A) 절반
    (B) 전체
    (C) 4분의 1

11. (A) 텅 빈
    (B) 가득 찬
    (C) 사라지다

12. (A) 해가 졌다.
    (B) 해가 떠오르고 있다.
    (C) 햇빛이 비치고 있다.

13. (A) 소녀는 나무 아래에서 책을 읽고 있다.
    (B) 소녀는 나무 아래에서 쉬고 있다.
    (C) 소녀는 나무 아래를 달리고 있다.

14. (A) 소년은 사진을 찍고 있다.
    (B) 소년은 야구를 하고 있다.
    (C) 소년은 통화를 하고 있다.

15. (A) 소녀는 벤치 위에 앉아 있다.
    (B) 소녀는 벤치 옆에 서 있다.
    (C) 소녀는 벤치에 누워 있다.

16. (A) 두 소녀가 휘파람을 불고 있다.
    (B) 소녀들은 화가 났다.
    (C) 한 소녀는 속삭이고 있다.

17. (A) 그들은 탁구를 치고 있다.
    (B) 그들은 테니스를 치고 있다.
    (C) 그들은 피구를 하고 있다.

18. (A) 뱀이 터널 위를 지나고 있다.
    (B) 뱀이 다리를 건너고 있다.
    (C) 뱀이 터널을 통과하고 있다.

Part 2.

19. 사람들은 좋은 냄새를 내기 위해 이것을 뿌립니다. 보통 액체이며 다양한 종류의 냄새가 납니다. 그 중 일부는 달콤하고 신선하며 꽃향기까지 납니다. 그것은 무엇일까요?

    (A) 땀
    (B) 눈물
    (C) 향수

20. 이것들은 학업을 하고, 동영상을 시청하고, 사람들과 소통하는 데 도움이 될 수 있습니다. 휴대가 간편하며 거의 모든 곳에서 사용할 수 있습니다. 이것들은 무엇일까요?

    (A) 노트북
    (B) 키보드
    (C) 라디오

21. 사람들은 이것에 물을 넣습니다. 이것은 물을 빠르게 끓이는 데 도움이 됩니다. 사람들은 이것을 사용하여 핫초코와 차를 만들 수 있습니다. 이것은 무엇일까요?

    (A) 텀블러
    (B) 플라스크
    (C) 주전자

22. 회사원들이 방에 모여 있습니다. 그들은 내년 계획에 대해 논의하고 있습니다. 어떤 사람들은 아이디어를 내고, 다른 사람들은 받아 적습니다.
    그들은 _____ 을/를 하는 중이다.

    (A) 회의
    (B) 집안일
    (C) 퍼즐

23. 사람들은 독서를 멈출 때 이걸 사용합니다. 보통 작고 종이나 플라스틱으로 만들어집니다. 책에서 읽던 위치를 표시하고 읽기를 멈춘 부분을 찾는데 도움이 될 수 있습니다. 그것은 무엇일까요?

    (A) 책꽂이
    (B) 책갈피
    (C) 소책자

24. 이 동물들은 길고 강한 4개 다리를 가지고 있습니다. 매우 빠르게 달릴 수 있고 사람들은 이것을 탈 수도 있습니다. 이것은 무엇일까요?

    (A) 사자
    (B) 캥거루
    (C) 말

25. 당신은 도서관에 있습니다. 마침내 역사 프로젝트에 필요한 책을 찾았습니다. 카운터로 가져갑니다.
    당신은 도서관에서 책을 _____ 중입니다.

    (A) 빌리다
    (B) 고르다
    (C) 운동하다

26. 이것은 사람들이 박테리아로부터 안전하게 보호하고 세균을 제거하는 데 도움이 됩니다. 사람들은 손을 씻을 수 없을 때 액체나 젤로 사용할 수 있습니다. 이것은 무엇일까요?

    (A) 손 소독제
    (B) 행커치프
    (C) 수갑

27. 소년은 부엌에서 엄마를 돕고 있습니다. 그는 접시, 포크, 칼을 들고 다이닝 룸으로 나갑니다. 그는 그것들을 식탁으로 가져갑니다. 그는 저녁을 위해 식탁을 _____ 하려고 한다.

    (A) 나타내다
    (B) 미루다
    (C) 차리다

Part 3.

[28-31] 아래를 읽고, 28-31번 질문에 답하세요.

\multicolumn{3}{c}{Westfield 학교 현장 학습 – 1학기 : 3월}		
시간	활동	장소
오전 7시 30분	학교에서 출발 – 오전 8시 – 학생들은 최소한 7시 45분까지 도착해야 함	학교 주차장
오전 9시	아쿠아리움 투어 – 사진 촬영은 금지되어 있음	시티 아쿠아리움
오후 12시	점심 – 점심은 직접 지참	시티 아쿠아리움 식당
오후 1시	해양동물에 대해 배우기 – 모든 학생은 필기해야 함 – 다음 주에 배운 내용에 대한 시험이 있을 예정임	시티 아쿠아리움 메인 홀
오후 5시	학교로 복귀	학교 주차장 – 도착시간 : 대략 오후 6시 30분

28. 학생들은 최소 몇 시까지 학교에 도착해야 합니까?

    (A) 오전 7시 30분
    (B) 오전 7시 45분
    (C) 오전 7시 50분

29. 현장 학습에 학생들은 무엇을 가져와야 합니까?

    (A) 카메라
    (B) 집에서 싸온 점심
    (C) 여분의 옷

30. 학생들은 어디서 점심을 먹습니까?

    (A) 식당에서
    (B) 메인 홀에서
    (C) 주차장에서

31. 현장 학습 일정은 주로 무엇에 관한 것입니까?

    (A) 학생들이 볼 수 있는 해양 생물의 목록
    (B) 어떻게 학생들이 아쿠아리움에 도착할 것인지
    (C) 현장 학습에서 무엇을 하게 될 예정인지

[32-35] 아래를 읽고, 32-35번 질문에 답하세요.

> **West Field 초등학교 현장 학습**
>
> **일자 :**
> 12월 23일 금요일 오전 9시, 학교 주차장
> (최소 30분 일찍 오세요)
> 장소 : 롤링 놀이공원
> 착용 : 다양한 활동을 즐길 수 있는 편안한 옷과 운동화
>
> **준비물 :**
> 수영복(수영을 할 경우), 물, 자외선 차단제, 음식과 간식을 위한 돈
>
> **활동**
> 모두를 위한 신나는 활동들이 많이 있을 것입니다!
>
> - 아이스 스케이팅장
>   빙상 위에서 스케이트를 탈 수 있는 기회를 즐기세요.
> - 롤러코스터
>   모두를 위한 스릴 넘치는 놀이기구(일부 놀이기구에는 연령 제한이 있음)
> - 워터파크
>   수영을 원한다면 수영복을 꼭 챙기기
> - 라이브 콘서트
>   신나는 공연을 보고 유명한 가수들 만나기
>
> **중요 공지**
> • 동의서
>   – 보호자의 서명이 있는 동의서를 담임 선생님께 제출해야 함
>   – 12월 2일 수요일까지 제출해야 함
> • 건강 관련 주의사항
>   – 자녀가 건강상의 문제가 있는 경우, 반드시 학교에 알려야 함

32. 학생들은 몇 시에 학교 주차장에 도착해야 하나요?

(A) 늦어도 오전 8시 30분까지
(B) 오전 9시에
(C) 오전 9시 30분경

33. 워터파크를 즐기고 싶다면 무엇을 가져가야 하나요?

(A) 자외선 차단제
(B) 물
(C) 수영복

34. 학생들이 편안한 옷을 입어야 하는 이유는 무엇입니까?

(A) 달리기 대회가 열릴 것입니다.
(B) 즐길 수 있는 활동이 많을 것입니다.
(C) 날씨가 매우 더울 것입니다.

35. 자녀에게 건강 문제가 있는 경우 부모는 무엇을 해야 하나요?

(A) 놀이공원에 동의서에 서명해 달라고 요청한다.
(B) 건강 상태에 대해 학교에 알린다.
(C) 담임 선생님께 이번 여행이 얼마나 신나는지 말한다.

[36-37] 이메일을 읽고, 36-37번 질문에 답하세요.

> 받는 사람: Stratford 미술관
> 보내는 사람: Granger 부인
> 주제: 학교 현장 학습에 관한 질문
>
> Stratford 미술관 팀에게,
>
> 저는 Martin International School의 강사이며 학생들을 미술관으로 현장 학습시키고 싶습니다. 학교에서 Pablo Picasso 에 대해 배우고 있는데 작가에 대한 특별 전시회가 열린다고 들었습니다. 전시회에 대해 자세히 알려주실 수 있나요? 또한 약 50명의 학생을 데려갈 예정인데 점심을 먹을 수 있는 공간이 있을까요?
> 시간 내주셔서 감사합니다. 답변 기다리겠습니다.
>
> 감사합니다.
> Granger 부인

36. Granger 부인이 묻지 않은 것은 무엇입니까?

(A) 학생들이 사진을 찍을 수 있는 장소
(B) 전시회에 대한 세부 정보
(C) 학생들이 점심을 먹을 수 있는 장소

37. Granger 부인은 왜 학생들을 미술관에 데려가고 싶어 하나요?

(A) 학생들이 그림을 배우기를 원해서
(B) 학생들이 예술가에 대해 더 많이 배우기를 원해서
(C) 학생들이 Pablo Picasso의 전시회를 만들기를 원해서

[38-39] 이메일을 읽고, 38-39번 질문에 답하세요.

> 받는 사람: 학생들
> 보내는 사람: Brown 선생님
> 주제: 현장 학습 알림
>
> 학생 여러분께,
>
> 다음 주에 있을 New Forest 현장학습을 기대하고 있기를 바랍니다. 여러분 모두에게 신나는 행사가 될 것이며 주변 풍경을 그릴 수 있는 좋은 기회가 될 것입니다.
> 다시 한번 준비물을 기억하세요. 연필, 지우개, 색연필을 꼭 챙기세요. 풍경을 그릴 예정이니 다양한 색연필을 가져오면 그림을 더욱 다채롭게 그릴 수 있습니다. 또한 도시락과 마실 것도 꼭 챙겨야 합니다.
> 월요일에 여러분 모두를 뵙기를 기대합니다!
>
> Brown 선생님

38. Brown 선생님은 왜 학생들에게 편지를 보냈습니까?

(A) 학생들에게 학교에 일찍 오라고 상기시키기 위해
(B) 월요일에 그림을 제출하도록 상기시키기 위해
(C) 학급 학생들에게 미술 용품을 가져오라고 상기시키기 위해

39. 학생들은 무엇을 그릴 예정입니까?

(A) 나무와 꽃
(B) 친구들
(C) 색연필

Listening

1 (A)	2 (B)	3 (C)	4 (A)
5 (B)	6 (C)	7 (A)	8 (A)
9 (C)	10 (A)	11 (B)	12 (A)
13 (A)	14 (C)	15 (A)	16 (B)
17 (A)	18 (B)	19 (B)	20 (B)
21 (A)	22 (C)	23 (A)	24 (A)
25 (C)	26 (B)	27 (C)	28 (B)
29 (C)	30 (B)	31 (C)	32 (B)
33 (C)	34 (A)	35 (B)	36 (A)
37 (B)	38 (A)	39 (B)	40 (B)
41 (C)			

Part 1.

1. The boy is helping his mother.

그 소년은 그의 어머니를 돕는 중이다.

2. The doctor is giving medicine.

그 의사는 약을 처방해주는 중이다.

3. The girl fell over.

그 소녀는 넘어졌다.

4. There are pictures on the cabinet.

캐비닛 위에 사진들이 있다.

5. The suitcase is almost full.

그 여행가방은 거의 꽉 찼다.

6. The jacket is too big for the girl.

그 소녀에게 자켓은 너무 크다.

7. The green team is cheering louder than the red team.

녹색팀이 빨간팀보다 크게 응원하고 있다.

Part 2.

8.
W: Listen to a girl.
G: Dad, look at that little girl on TV. She is upside down. She must be in gym class.
W: What is the girl asking her father to see?

W: 소녀가 하는 얘기를 들어보세요.
G: 아빠, TV에 나오는 저 작은 소녀 좀 봐요. 그녀는 물구나무를 섰어요. 체육 수업을 듣나봐요.
W: 딸이 아빠에게 무엇을 보라고 하고 있나요?

9.
W: Listen to a father.
M: Kids, your mom and I are going away for the long weekend. You'll be staying at Grandma and Grandpa's house.
W: What did the father tell his children they would do?

W: 아빠의 얘기를 들어보세요.
M: 얘들아, 너희 엄마와 나는 긴 주말 연휴에 여행을 갈 거야. 너희는 할머니와 할아버지 댁에 머물 거야.
W: 아빠는 자녀들에게 무엇을 하겠다고 말했습니까?

10.
W: Listen to a teacher in a science class.
W: Now, put your egg into a glass of water. Yes, it sinks. But here comes the exciting part. Take the egg out, add some salt to the water, and then put the egg back in. The egg rises to the top and floats!
W: What did the teacher tell her students to do?

W: 과학 수업에서 선생님의 얘기를 들어보세요.
W: 이제 달걀을 물이 담긴 유리잔에 넣어 보세요. 네, 가라앉죠. 그런데 흥미로운 부분은 지금부터예요. 달걀을 꺼내고, 물에 소금을 넣은 다음, 다시 달걀을 넣어 보세요. 그러면 달걀이 위로 떠오릅니다!
W: 선생님은 학생들에게 무엇을 하라고 했나요?

11.
W: Listen to a boy.
B: Everyone! I have a surprise! My father is a fisherman. He is here to give a presentation about a fisherman's life. He needs a large space, so it will take place in the assembly hall. Let's go there!
W: What did the boy ask his friends to do?

W: 소년의 얘기를 들어보세요.
B: 얘들아! 깜짝 놀랄 일이 있어! 우리 아빠는 어부이신데 어부의 삶에 대한 발표를 해주시려고 여기 오셨어. 넓은 자리가 필요해서, 대강당에서 진행될 거야. 같이 가보자!
W: 소년은 친구들에게 무엇을 요청했습니까?

12.
W: Listen to a photographer.
M: It's time for our class picture. Boys, please stand in the back. Girls, you stand in the front. Everyone, smile and say cheese. This picture will be in our school yearbook. Ready? 3,2,1! Click!
W: What did the photographer ask the children to do?

W: 사진작가의 얘기를 들어보세요.
M: 이제 우리 반 사진을 찍을 시간입니다. 남학생들, 뒤에 서 주세요. 여학생들, 앞에 서세요. 모두 웃으며 치즈라고 말하세요. 이 사진은 우리 학교 졸업 앨범에 실릴 거예요. 준비됐어요? 3, 2, 1! 찰칵!
W: 사진작가가 아이들에게 무엇을 요청했습니까?

13.
W: Listen to a mother.
W: OK, John. Today Uncle Thomas will visit us and we are going to have dinner together. Make sure you are home in time for dinner. Now, before you go, can you put the saucepan on the table, please?
W: What did the mother tell her son to do?

W: 엄마의 얘기를 들어보세요.
W: John. 오늘 Thomas 삼촌이 방문해서 저녁을 함께 먹을 거야. 저녁 식사 시간에 맞춰 집에 도착해야 해. 가기 전에 냄비를 테이블 위에 올려주겠니?
W: 엄마는 아들에게 무엇을 하라고 했습니까?

14.
W: Listen to an uncle.
M: Peter, can you please walk this down to the post office? The address is on it but it needs stamps and I need the receipt. It's just a local address so you don't need to fill out any customs forms. Can you go now?
W: What did the uncle ask his nephew to do?

W: 삼촌의 얘기를 들어보세요.
M: Peter, 이걸 우체국에 가져다 줄 수 있겠니? 주소는 적혀 있지만 우표랑 영수증이 필요해. 국내 주소라서 세관 서류를 작성할 필요가 없단다. 지금 갈 수 있니?
W: 삼촌은 조카에게 무엇을 부탁했나요?

15.
W: Listen to a mother.
W: Harry, I know you love science, but you need to finish your social studies report first. You can't watch science fiction cartoons now. Please turn off the T.V. and finish your report. You told me you have to hand it in by tomorrow. You can watch the cartoons after finishing the social studies report.
W: What did the mother tell her son to do?

W: 엄마의 얘기를 들어보세요.
W: Harry, 과학을 좋아하는 건 알지만 사회과목 보고서를 먼저 끝내야 한단다. 지금은 공상과학 만화를 볼 수 없어. TV를 끄고 보고서를 끝내렴. 내일까지 제출해야 하잖니. 사회과목 보고서를 마친 후에 만화를 보렴.
W: 엄마는 아들에게 무엇을 하라고 얘기했나요?

16.
W: Listen to a gym teacher.
M: The school Sports Day has been changed from May 15th to July 20th. You have an extra three months, which will give you more time to practice. So please cross out May 15th and circle July 20th on your calendar. On the Sports Day our class is going to play soccer and badminton.
W: What did the gym teacher tell his students to do?

W: 체육 선생님의 얘기를 들어보세요.
M: 학교 운동회가 5월 15일에서 7월 20일로 변경되었습니다. 3개월이 더 생겼으니 연습할 시간이 더 많을 거예요. 그러니 달력에 5월 15일에 선을 그어 지우고 7월 20일에 동그라미로 표시하세요. 운동회날에 우리 반은 축구와 배드민턴을 할 예정입니다.
W: 체육 선생님은 학생들에게 무엇을 하라고 얘기했나요?

17.
W: Listen to a school bus driver.
M: Everyone, this is the last stop. We've arrived at our destination. Everyone should get off the bus now. Please make sure to take all your belongings with you.
W: What did the school bus driver tell the students to do?

W: 스쿨버스 운전기사의 얘기를 들어보세요.
M: 여러분, 여기가 마지막 정류장입니다. 목적지에 도착했습니다. 이제 모두 버스에서 내려야 합니다. 모든 소지품을 꼭 챙기세요.
W: 스쿨버스 운전기사가 학생들에게 무엇을 하라고 얘기했나요?

Part 3.

18.
W: How much does this painting cost?
(A) It's very colorful.
(B) It's a little expensive.
(C) It looks great on the wall.

W: 이 그림의 가격은 얼마입니까?
(A) 매우 다채롭습니다.
(B) 조금 비쌉니다.
(C) 벽에 잘 어울립니다.

[19-21] Listen to a girl talking to her friend.
소녀가 친구에게 하는 얘기를 들어보세요.

19. G: How was the soccer game last night?

(A) I can't find my ticket.
(B) I couldn't go yesterday.
(C) I can't find my camera.

G: 어젯밤 축구 경기 어땠니?

(A) 티켓을 못 찾겠어.
(B) 어제는 갈 수 없었어.
(C) 카메라를 못 찾겠어.

20. G: Did you hear which team won the game?

(A) All soccer teams are great.
(B) I heard it was a tie.
(C) I heard that it was a big stadium.

G: 어느 팀이 이겼는지 들었니?

(A) 모든 축구팀은 훌륭해.
(B) 동점이라고 들었어.
(C) 큰 경기장이라고 들었어.

21. G: How about we check out the match tomorrow?

(A) That sounds like a plan.
(B) There's no game tonight.
(C) I'm sorry you were sick yesterday.

G: 내일 경기를 보러 가는 게 어때?

(A) 그거 좋은 계획인 것 같아.
(B) 오늘 밤에는 경기가 없어.
(C) 어제 아팠다니 유감이다.

[22-24] Listen to a boy talking to his father.
소년이 아빠에게 하는 얘기를 들어보세요.

22. B: Can I go to summer camp again next year?

(A) Yes, it's been a long time.
(B) Good idea, I know how much you like to ice skate.
(C) We'll have to see, but it sounds like you had so much fun.

B: 내년에 다시 여름 캠프에 갈 수 있을까요?

(A) 응, 오랜만이구나.
(B) 좋은 생각이야, 네가 아이스 스케이트를 얼마나 좋아하는지 안단다.
(C) 한번 생각해보자. 그래도 정말 재미있게 보낸 것 같구나.

23. M: What was the most exciting experience?

(A) Making team flags
(B) It was a lot of work
(C) Coming back home

M: 가장 재밌는 경험은 무엇이었니?

(A) 팀 깃발을 만든 것
(B) 정말 많은 일이었어
(C) 집으로 돌아가는 길

24. B: Can I visit my friend I met at camp this week?

(A) Only if you finish all your homework first.
(B) I think visiting the camp is the best choice.
(C) I thought it was last week.

B: 제가 이번주에 캠프에서 만난 친구를 만나도 될까요?

(A) 네가 숙제를 먼저 끝내면 가도 된단다.
(B) 캠프에 방문하는게 가장 좋은 것 같단다.
(C) 나는 그것이 저번 주 인 줄 알았다.

Part 4.

25. W: Listen to a conversation between a mother and her daughter. Listen for the answer to this question.

G: Mom, can I have a sleepover this weekend?
W: How about next week instead?
G: I thought we were going to grandma's next week.
W: Change of plans, we're going on Friday and coming back next Monday.

W: When will the girl have a sleepover?

W: 엄마와 딸 사이의 대화를 듣고 질문에 답하세요.

G: 엄마, 이번 주말에 친구 불러서 같이 자도 될까요?
W: 대신 다음 주는 어떠니?
G: 다음 주에 할머니 댁에 가는 줄 알았어요.
W: 계획이 변경되어서 금요일에 갔다가 다음 주 월요일에 돌아올 예정이란다.

W: 소녀는 언제 친구를 초대해서 잘 예정인가요?

(A) 금요일
(B) 이번 주말
(C) 다음 주말

26. W: Listen to a conversation between two students at school. Listen for the answer to this question.

G: What are you reading?
B: A book about people in Switzerland, I have to finish a project about Swiss people by Friday.

G: Oh, I love studying other countries.
B: Me, too. The Swiss people are fascinating. Did you know Albert Einstein lived in Switzerland for a while? He studied and taught science there.
G: Really?
W: What subject is the boy doing a project for?

W: 학교에서 두 학생 사이의 대화를 듣고 질문에 답하세요.

G: 무엇을 읽고 있니?
B: 스위스 사람들에 관한 책이야. 금요일까지 스위스 사람들에 대한 프로젝트를 끝내야 해.
G: 아, 나는 다른 나라에 대해 공부하는 것을 정말 좋아해.
B: 나도. 스위스 사람들은 정말 매력적이야. Albert Einstein이 한동안 스위스에서 살았다는 걸 알고 있어? 그는 그곳에서 과학을 공부하고 가르쳤어.
G: 정말?

W: 소년은 어떤 과목으로 프로젝트를 진행하고 있습니까?

(A) 과학
(B) 사회
(C) 수학

27.
W: Listen to a conversation between a boy and his coach. Listen for the answer to this question.
M: Everyone, please be out in the baseball field in ten minutes.
B: Coach Martin, I think I left my baseball shirt at home. I can't find it anywhere.
M: Are you sure, Alex? Didn't you also forget to bring your shirt last week?
B: It was my shorts last week. Sorry, Coach.
M: Alex, you must remember to check if you have everything before coming to school.
B: I thought I checked, but I guess I didn't look properly.
M: Can you go around the class and ask one of your friends to lend you one?
B: OK, thank you, Coach.
M: Sure, but don't forget your shirt next time.
W: What does Coach Martin tell Alex to do?

W: 소년과 그의 코치 사이의 대화를 듣고 질문에 답하세요.

M: 여러분, 10분 후에 야구장으로 나와 주세요.
B: Martin 코치님, 야구 셔츠를 집에 두고 온 것 같아요. 어디에서도 찾을 수가 없네요.
M: Alex, 확실하니? 지난주에도 셔츠 가져오는 것을 잊지 않았니?
B: 지난주에는 제 반바지였어요. 죄송합니다, 코치님.
M: Alex, 학교에 오기 전에 모든 것을 챙겼는지 꼭 확인해야 해.
B: 확인한 줄 알았는데 제대로 보지 않았나 봐요.

M: 그럼 반을 돌아다니면서 친구한테 셔츠를 빌릴 수 있는지 물어볼래?
B: 네, 감사합니다, 코치님.
M: 다음번에는 셔츠를 잊지 마렴.

W: Martin 코치가 Alex에게 무엇을 하라고 했나요?

(A) 집에 가서 야구 셔츠를 가지러 가기
(B) 가능한 한 빨리 야구장에 나가기
(C) 친구들에게 야구 셔츠를 빌리기

28.
W: Listen to a conversation between a father and his son. Listen for the answer to this question.
B: Dad, I learned in school that chocolate can be good for our health.
M: It sure can. What did you learn?
B: I learned that dark chocolate can help our heart, and even boost our moods.
M: That's right. What else did you learn?
B: It even helps our brain. It helps to enhance our memories and stay focused in school.
But, it's also important to not eat too much of it.
M: Yes, if we don't brush our teeth properly, we might get cavities.
B: Exactly, and some people might gain weight, since it's high in calories.
M: That's right. It's important to not overeat it.
W: What is NOT a benefit of chocolate?

W: 아빠와 아들 사이의 대화를 듣고 질문에 답하세요.

B: 아빠, 학교에서 초콜릿이 건강에 좋을 수 있다는 것을 배웠어요.
M: 그럴 수 있지. 무엇을 배웠니?
B: 다크 초콜릿이 심장에 도움이 되고 기분을 좋게 할 수도 있다는 것을 배웠어요.
M: 맞아. 또 무엇을 배웠니?
B: 뇌에도 도움이 된대요. 기억력을 향상시키고 학교에서 집중하는 데 도움이 된대요.
하지만 너무 많이 먹지 않는 것도 중요해요.
M: 맞아, 양치질을 제대로 하지 않으면 충치가 생길 수 있어.
B: 맞아요, 그리고 칼로리가 높아서 어떤 사람들은 살이 찔 수도 있어요.
M: 맞아. 과식하지 않는 것이 중요하단다.

W: 초콜릿의 장점이 아닌 것은 무엇인가요?

(A) 심장 건강을 개선할 수 있다.
(B) 충치를 유발할 수 있다.
(C) 우리의 기분을 좋게 만들 수 있다.

29.

W: Listen to a conversation between a boy and his teacher. Listen for the answer to this question.

M: Hello? This is Mr. Brown from Pine Heights Elementary School. Could I talk to Kevin, please?

B: Hi, Mr. Brown. It's me Kevin.

M: Oh, hi Kevin, I just wanted to let you know that tomorrow's soccer practice has been cancelled. There is going to be a heavy snowfall tonight.

B: Oh no! Dad did tell me about the snowfall though. So, when can we practice?

M: I was thinking Saturday. I know that we don't usually have practice on the weekends, but I think we need to since it's the start of the tournament soon.

B: Yeah, I'm actually really nervous about it. Saturday works fine for me. Should I tell the team about the reschedule?

M: No, it's OK. I'll be sending an email to the team now. I wanted to let you know first since you're the team captain.

B: Right, thanks, Mr. Brown.

W: Why did Mr. Brown call Kevin?

W: 소년과 선생님 사이의 대화를 듣고 질문에 답하세요.

M: 여보세요? Pine Heights 초등학교의 Brown 선생님입니다. Kevin과 통화할 수 있을까요?

B: 안녕하세요, 선생님. 저 Kevin이에요.

M: 안녕, Kevin. 내일 축구 연습이 취소되었단다. 오늘 밤 폭설이 내릴 예정이래.

B: 안돼! 아빠가 눈 소식에 대해 말씀해 주셨어요. 그럼 언제 연습할 수 있을까요?

M: 토요일을 생각하고 있단다. 보통 주말에 연습이 없지만 곧 대회가 시작되기 때문에 연습이 필요할 것 같아.

B: 네, 사실 정말 긴장돼요. 저는 토요일 괜찮은데, 팀에게 일정 변경에 대해 알려야 할까요?

M: 아니, 괜찮아. 지금 팀에 이메일을 보낼거야. 네가 팀의 주장이니 먼저 알려주려 했단다.

B: 네, 감사합니다, 선생님.

W: Brown 선생님은 왜 케빈에게 전화를 했습니까?

(A) 축구 대회 일정이 변경되었다고 그에게 말하기 위해

(B) 그에게 그의 아버지가 눈 오는 것에 대해 말해줬다고 말하기 위해

(C) 토요일에 연습할 시간이 있는지 묻기 위해

30.

W: Listen to a conversation between two friends. Listen for the answer to this question.

G: Wow, did you see that planet? I wonder what it is.

B: That's Mars. It looks extraordinary.

G: Are you sure? It looks like Jupiter to me.

B: Do you see that the color is reddish orange? That's the color of Mars. Jupiter looks yellowish-brown, you see.

G: I didn't know that! What else?

B: Hmm, well the size is completely different too. Even through a telescope, Mars can look very small, but when you see Jupiter, I bet you'll be very surprised at how big it is.

G: It's so interesting. I love looking through telescopes. We can see things that are so far away.

B: I agree, it's like a magnifying glass. Without one, everything looks like a tiny dot.

G: It does! I can't wait to tell dad everything I saw!

W: What did the students see with a telescope?

W: 두 친구 사이의 대화를 듣고 질문에 답하세요.

G: 와, 저 행성 봤어? 무슨 행성인지 궁금하다.

B: 저건 화성이야. 정말 멋져.

G: 정말? 내 눈에는 목성처럼 보여.

B: 붉은 주황색이 보이니? 그게 화성의 색이야. 목성은 보다시피 황갈색으로 보여.

G: 몰랐어! 또 뭐가 있니?

B: 음, 크기도 완전히 달라. 망원경을 통해도 화성은 매우 작아 보이지만 목성을 보면 너는 목성의 크기에 매우 놀랄 거야.

G: 정말 흥미롭다. 나는 망원경을 통해 행성을 보는 것을 좋아해. 우리는 아주 멀리 있는 것들을 볼 수 있어.

B: 나도 동의해. 망원경은 마치 돋보기 같아. 돋보기가 없으면 모든 것이 작은 점처럼 보이잖아.

G: 맞아! 아빠에게 내가 본 모든 것을 빨리 말해주고 싶어!

W: 학생들은 망원경으로 무엇을 보았나요?

(A) 목성

(B) 화성

(C) 돋보기

31.

W: Listen to a conversation between two siblings. Listen for the answer to this question.

G: How about we walk to school today instead of taking mom's car?

B: It's a long way to walk. The last time, it took me an hour.

G: Then, how about we use public transportation?

B: Sounds good. How does taking the bus sound?

G: Well, it's rush hour soon, and I think there'll be traffic.

B: You're right. Then the subway?

G: Good idea. We should do what we can to protect the Earth.

B: I agree. It's the little things we do that help save the environment.

W: How are the students getting to school?

W: 두 남매 사이의 대화를 듣고 질문에 답하세요.

G: 오늘 엄마 차를 타지 않고 걸어서 학교에 가는 게 어때?

B: 걷기에는 먼 거리야. 지난번에는 한 시간이 걸렸잖아.

G: 그럼 대중교통을 이용하는 건 어떨까?

B: 좋아. 버스를 타는 게 어때?

G: 곧 러시아워라서 교통 체증이 있을 것 같아.

B: 맞네, 그럼 지하철은 어때?

G: 좋은 생각이야. 우리는 지구를 보호하기 위해 할 수 있는 일을 해야 해.

B: 나도 동의해. 우리가 하는 작은 행동들이 환경을 지키는데 도움이 돼.

W: 학생들은 학교에 어떻게 가고 있나요?

(A) 걸어서

(B) 버스를 타고

(C) 지하철을 타고

32.

W: Listen to a conversation between a mother and her son. Listen for the answer to this question.

B: Mom, we checked in, our passports were cleared, and now we've been waiting for over two hours to get on the plane! Grandma and Grandpa will be worried.

W: Yes, I know, dear. They just announced that the plane is having a last-minute mechanical check of the engine. They probably won't be much longer.

B: Oh, mom, I'm hungry.

W: You'll need to wait until we are on the plane. Oh, there's the announcement now! We will be boarding in 5 minutes. Grab your things.

B: It's about time!

W: Why did the mother and son have to wait so long in the boarding area?

W: 엄마와 아들 사이의 대화를 듣고 질문에 답하세요.

B: 엄마, 체크인하고 여권 심사도 마쳤는데, 비행기 타려고 두 시간 넘게 기다리고 있어요! 할머니와 할아버지가 걱정하실 거예요.

W: 알고 있단다. 방금 비행기가 엔진에 대한 막바지 점검을 하고 있다고 안내 했어. 아마 더 시간이 걸리지 않을 거란다.

B: 아, 엄마, 배고파요.

W: 비행기에 탑승할 때까지 기다려야 해. 아, 이제 안내 방송이 나오네! 5분 후에 탑승할 예정이야. 짐을 챙기렴.

B: 드디어 타네요!

W: 엄마와 아들은 왜 탑승 구역에서 오래 기다려야 했습니까?

(A) 건강 검진을 받아야 했기 때문에

(B) 비행기가 엔진 점검을 받고 있었기 때문에

(C) 음식이 오기를 기다리고 있었기 때문에

33.

W: Listen to a conversation between two students. Listen for the answer to this question.

B: Do you know what chapters we have to read for history class?

G: Yes! But the problem is that the history books the teacher asked us to read are all taken out. There are none left in the school library.

B: Are you sure? They were there when I went yesterday.

G: I'm positive. I even asked the librarian if any books were left.

B: I think that a lot of students went to borrow the book before us.

G: Then, how about we check out the local library?

B: That sounds like a plan! But my library card is at home.

G: All right, let's go and get it first.

W: Where will the students go next?

W: 두 학생 사이의 대화를 듣고 질문에 답하세요.

B: 역사 수업을 위해 어떤 챕터를 읽어야 하는지 아니?

G: 응! 그런데 문제는 선생님이 읽으라고 한 역사책이 모두 대출 되었다는 거야. 학교 도서관에는 없어.

B: 정말? 어제 갔을 때는 거기 있었어.

G: 확실해, 사서 선생님에게 책이 남아 있는지 물어보기도 했어.

B: 많은 학생들이 우리보다 먼저 책을 빌리러 간 것 같아.

G: 그럼, 우리 동네 도서관에 가보는 건 어때?

B: 좋은 계획이다! 근데 내 도서관 카드가 집에 있어.

G: 좋아, 먼저 그것부터 가지러 가자.

W: 학생들은 어디로 갈까요?

(A) 공공 도서관

(B) 학교 도서관

(C) 그 소년의 집

Part 5.

34.

W: Hey, Daisy. You forgot to take your lunch today to school. Do you want me to bring it to you? Call me, so I can drop it off before going to the department store.

W: Why did mom call Daisy?

W: 안녕, Daisy. 오늘 점심을 학교에 가져가는 것을 잊었더라. 내가 가져다줄까? 백화점에 가기 전에 도시락을 가져다줄 수 있으니까, 전화 주렴.

W: 엄마가 Daisy에게 왜 전화를 했습니까?

(A) 도시락이 필요한지 확인하기 위해

(B) 백화점에 가기 전에 그녀에게 전화하라고 하기 위해

(C) 백화점에서 필요한 것이 있는지 확인하기 위해

35.
G: Sally, hey, it's Julie. I can't wait for the sleepover tonight. I got the chocolates and marshmallows like you asked. Is there anything else you need help with? Call me back!

W: Why did Julie call?

G: Sally, 안녕. 나 Julie야. 오늘 밤 자고 오는거 너무 기대 돼. 네가 부탁한 초콜릿이랑 마시멜로도 챙겼어. 다른 도움이 필요한 것이 있니? 전화 줘!

W: Julie는 왜 전화했나요?

(A) Sally가 자고 오는 것을 얼마나 기대하고 있는지 말하기 위해
(B) 그녀가 더 할 수 있는 일이 있는지 알아보기 위해
(C) Sally를 슬립 오버에 초대하기 위해

36.
M: Hi Jake, it's Coach Miller. We'll be having a new player in our team on Monday and I wanted to let you know first. His name is Kevin and he's the same age as you. Since you're the team captain, can you introduce Kevin to the members on your team? I think getting to know him first will help before practice on Tuesday.

W: What did Coach Miller ask Jake to do?

M: 안녕 Jake, Miller 코치란다. 월요일에 새로운 선수가 팀에 합류할 예정인데 먼저 알려주고 싶었단다. 그의 이름은 Kevin이고 너와 동갑이란다. 팀 주장이니 팀원들에게 Kevin을 소개해 줄 수 있니? 화요일 연습 전에 그와 먼저 친해지는게 도움이 될 거야.

W: Miller 코치는 Jake에게 무엇을 요청했나요?

(A) Kevin이 팀원들과 친해지도록 도와주기
(B) Kevin에게 새로운 코치를 소개하기
(C) Kevin이 팀 주장이 된 것을 축하하기

37.
B: Hello, Mr. Thompson, it's Tom. Graduation is coming up, and I wanted to take this opportunity to thank you for all that you have done for our class this year. We appreciate you being the best teacher one could ever ask for. My classmates and I want to throw a party for you this Friday after school. I know you're busy because it's the end of the school year, but please tell me if Friday works for you.

W: What did Tom call about?

B: 안녕하세요, Thompson 선생님. Tom입니다. 곧 졸업이 다가오네요. 이번 기회를 빌어 올 한 해 동안 우리 반을 위해 애써주신 것에 대해 감사드리고 싶습니다. 최고의 선생님이 되어주셔서 감사합니다. 저희 반 친구들과 저는 이번 금요일 방과 후에 선생님을 위해 파티를 열고 싶어요. 학기 말이라 바쁘시겠지만 금요일이 괜찮으시면 말씀해 주세요.

W: Tom은 무슨 일로 전화했나요?

(A) 졸업식
(B) 감사 파티
(C) 감사 편지

38.
W: Kylie, it's Mrs. Turner. I just wanted to let you know that you need to bring a raincoat for the trip. It might rain a little tomorrow, and we don't want to be wandering around wet.

W: Why did Mrs. Turner call?

W: Kylie, Turner 부인이란다. 여행을 위해 비옷을 가져가야 한다는 것을 알려주고 싶었단다. 내일 비가 조금 올 수도 있고, 젖은 채로 돌아다니고 싶지 않거든.

W: Turner 부인은 왜 전화를 했습니까?

(A) 비 올 때 입을 옷을 가져오라고 말하기 위해
(B) 감기에 걸리고 싶지 않다고 말하기 위해
(C) 비 때문에 여행이 취소되었다고 그녀에게 말하기 위해

39.
W: Good morning, Kelly. It's mom. I tried to get your violin strings tuned, but it seems that the strings are too old. I ordered a new set of strings for you today, and it's going to arrive in two weeks. In the meantime, I asked your violin teacher if she could lend you a spare one until it arrives. Please make sure to call and thank her.

W: What did mom call about?

W: 좋은 아침, Kelly. 엄마야. 바이올린 줄을 조율해 보려고 했는데 줄이 너무 오래된 것 같아. 오늘 새 줄 셋트를 주문했는데 2주 후에 도착할 예정이라는구나. 네 바이올린 선생님께 줄이 도착할 때까지 여분의 줄을 빌려주실 수 있는지 여쭤보았으니 꼭 전화해서 감사 인사를 전하렴.

W: 엄마는 무슨 일로 전화했나요?

(A) 오늘 새 바이올린을 가져가라고 상기시키기 위해
(B) 바이올린 선생님께 잊지 않고 전화하여 감사 인사를 드리기 위해
(C) 그녀에게 바이올린 줄을 2주 안에 조율할 수 있다고 말하기 위해

40.
M: This is Brian calling from the electronic store. We noticed that you bought a new laptop from our store last week. To celebrate our 30th anniversary, we decided to give free mouse pads to all our customers who purchased a computer this month. Please bring your receipt and come and get a free pad!

W: Why did Brian from the electronic store call?

M: 전자제품 매장 직원 Brian입니다. 지난주에 저희 매장에서 새 노트북을 구입하신 것을 확인했습니다. 창립 30주년을 기념하여 이번 달에 컴퓨터를 구매하신 모든 고객님께 마우스 패드를 무료로 증정하기로 했습니다. 영수증을 지참하시고 오셔서 무료 패드를 받아가세요!

W: 전자제품 매장의 Brian이 왜 전화를 했습니까?

(A) 환불을 요청하기 위해
(B) 무료 선물에 대한 소식을 공유하기 위해
(C) 새로운 노트북을 돌려주기 위해

41.
M: Hi Meredith, it's dad. I just got a call from your swimming coach saying that the competition has been delayed for two weeks. She asked if you can call her when you get home. Hope you have a great day, see you at home.

W: Why did Meredith's dad call?

M: 안녕, Meredith, 아빠란다. 방금 수영 코치님으로부터 대회가 2주 연기되었다는 전화를 받았어. 코치님이 네가 집에 오면 전화 달라고 하셨단다. 좋은 하루 되길 바라며, 집에서 보자.

W: Meredith의 아빠는 왜 전화를 했습니까?

(A) 집에 도착하면 아빠에게 전화하라고 하기 위해
(B) 대회가 앞당겨질 거라고 말하기 위해
(C) 수영 코치에게 전화하라고 하기 위해

Ace the TOEFL Primary Step 1